Eliminating corporal punishment

A human rights imperative
for Europe's children

2nd edition

The Council of Europe programme "Building a Europe for and with children"

www.coe.int/children

Council of Europe Publishing

French edition:
L'abolition des châtiments corporels – Un impératif pour les droits de l'enfant en Europe

ISBN 978-92-871-6268-7

This new, fully revised edition has been prepared by the Council of Europe programme "Building a Europe for and with children". This edition would not have been possible without the invaluable research skills of the Global Initiative to End All Corporal Punishment of Children.

Cover design: Graphic Design Studio, Council of Europe
Layout: Editions européennes

Council of Europe Publishing
F-67075 Strasbourg Cedex
http://book.coe.int

ISBN 978-92-871-6182-6
© Council of Europe, 2005
New edition December 2007
Printed in Belgium

Contents

*There are four additional online appendices. See "Reader's guide"
on p. 15.*

Foreword

"A little slap cannot do any harm" is the line often used by those defending the right of parents to use violence to discipline their children. Let's not forget that very similar language has been used in the past to condone domestic violence, nowadays unacceptable.

By the end of October 2007, 17 out of 47 Council of Europe member states had legally banned corporal punishment of children at home, at school, in care institutions or in places of detention.* This means that children in 30 European countries are not legally protected against the violation of their physical and psychological integrity.

The European Convention on Human Rights provides that "everyone" within the jurisdiction of a member state of the Council of Europe shall enjoy the rights and freedoms contained therein, including the right not to be subject to torture or inhuman and degrading treatment or punishment. There is no footnote in the Convention saying that children are excluded from the term "everyone". Therefore, children are protected as much as adults from violations of their fundamental rights.

True, progress has been made, but far too slow. Taking action against corporal punishment can be unpopular with the public and politicians. To some, it means challenging established traditions; most adults experienced corporal punishment when they were children themselves. They tend to see hitting, slapping and spanking as time-honoured methods of discipline. In reality, children rarely remember why they were hit, only belittlement and anxiety remain, and most

---

* Editor's note: In October 2007 Portugal became the 17th Council of Europe member state to initiate a total ban on corporal punishment of children. This change came about too late to be reflected in the main body of this book, which presents the situation as of June 2007.

corporal punishment is due to overstressed parents who have simply lost control.

For others, challenging corporal punishment means challenging family authority. The arguments of advocates of corporal punishment abound in clichés about the "sacred" and "inviolable" nature of the family space.

The number of parents and educators denouncing corporal punishment has risen since 1979, when Sweden initiated the first total ban in Europe. The Swedish example (and other countries which have since followed) has clearly shown us that public attitudes can be changed. Sweden accompanied its new law with awareness-raising campaigns. Educational pamphlets were sent to all households and schools to ensure that children themselves were aware of the new law protecting their rights. The results have been a clear decline in corporal punishment and the public belief in its benefits.

In early 2008, the Council of Europe programme "Building a Europe for and with children" will launch the first Europe-wide information activity against corporal punishment and in favour of positive parenting. It will focus on the ill-effects of corporal punishment based on the view of a predominant majority of child psychiatrists and psychologists and concentrate on the benefits of non-violent means of discipline.

Lifting the veil on this hidden issue should help to overcome several misconceptions and stereotypes which are often used by those who condone force to control children. Some of these are: positive parenting means permissive parenting; more parents will be sent to jail and children removed from their parents' home; and the state will now dictate how children should be raised.

All forms of physical punishment of children are a violation of basic human rights. These rights, protected by the European Convention on Human Rights, the European Social Charter and the United Nations Convention of the Rights of the Child, belong to children and adults. We care for children and help them to develop, but we do not own them. As guardians of their well-being, we have a legal and moral responsibility to provide them with a childhood which honours their rights and leaves them with a legacy which does not condone violence. Only when this happens will Europe become a true home for children.

The target date set by the United Nations for the total abolition of corporal punishment in Europe is 2009 and the forthcoming Council of Europe action should help us meet this goal.

Maud de Boer-Buquicchio

Deputy Secretary General of the Council of Europe

Summary

Hitting and humiliating children remains a very common form of punishment in a majority of the member states of the Council of Europe. About 30% of Europe's children live in states that have effective prohibition of all corporal punishment.

In many European countries, corporal punishment by parents remains lawful and socially approved. Research reveals that a majority of children are hit, including babies and very young children. Many are hit frequently – daily or more often – and implements are often used, such as belts, sticks and shoes. The fundamental human rights of millions of Europe's smallest and most vulnerable citizens are being breached on a large scale by those with the responsibility to love and care for them.

Human rights obligations

The Council of Europe is based on the principles of respect for the rule of law and enjoyment by all peoples of human rights and fundamental freedoms. Upon ratification of the European Convention on Human Rights and the European Social Charter or revised European Social Charter, the 47 member states of the Council take on binding obligations to respect the human rights of all people within their jurisdictions.

Judgments of the European Court of Human Rights have successively condemned corporal punishment of children in penal systems, schools and most recently in the home; other decisions have emphasised that banning all corporal punishment does not breach family privacy or religious rights. The European Committee of Social Rights, monitoring conformity with the European Social Charter, requires member states to reform their law to prohibit all corporal punishment and other humiliating treatment or punishment of children. The Committee of Ministers has condemned corporal punishment and proposed prohibition in a series of recommendations dating back to 1985. In 2006, it issued a recommendation calling on member states to create the conditions for positive parenting in the best interests of the child. Non-violent positive parenting is approached in the context of respect for and implementation of human rights (Appendix II). The Parliamentary Assembly in 2004 called for action to turn Europe into a corporal punishment free zone in its Recommendation 1666 (Appendix I). The Commissioner for Human Rights re-emphasised the human rights basis for prohibiting and eliminating all corporal punishment through legislative and other measures in the issue paper "The right not to be hit – also a children's right".

All member states have ratified the United Nations Convention on the Rights of the Child (UNCRC). This convention includes the obligation to protect children from all forms of physical or mental violence while in the care of parents and others. The monitoring body for the UNCRC, the Committee on the Rights of the Child (CRC), consistently interprets the convention as requiring the elimination of all corporal punishment, including in the home. The committee confirmed this in a general comment adopted in June 2006 on "The right of the child to protection from corporal punishment and other cruel or degrading forms of punishment (Articles 19; 28, para. 2; and 37, inter alia)" (see pp. 36-42). This provides detailed guidance to member states on fulfilling their obligations. Other international instruments also demand action against corporal punishment.

Progress towards abolition

By 2007, corporal punishment had been explicitly abolished in most member states in schools and in penal systems, albeit with varying levels of enforcement. In most countries it has also been prohibited in all institutions for children, but not consistently in other forms of alternative care.

Reform to remove parents' right to use corporal punishment began in the Nordic countries in the 1950s. By June 2007, at least 16 member states had introduced explicit legislation to prohibit all corporal punishment of children. In some but not all of these states, law reform has been accompanied by comprehensive awareness-raising and public education, aimed at ensuring that all children enjoy their rights to protection; where this has happened, research suggests that attitudes and practice can change very positively and quickly.

In some of the remaining 31 states, legislation still includes a specific defence for parents and other carers who use corporal punishment. In other countries the law is silent, but – in the absence of explicit prohibition – parental corporal punishment remains socially and legally approved. In two states, high-level court judgments have ruled against the use of corporal punishment in child-rearing, but in April 2006 a subsequent ruling in one of these states overturned the prohibition, illustrating the weakness of a prohibition that is not enshrined in legislation.

By early 2007, another seven member states had committed themselves to explicit law reform: see Appendix 1-online.

Action needed

The human rights obligations of member states require them to ensure that their law prohibits all corporal punishment and other degrading or humiliating treatment or punishment of children. In addition, they are responsible for ensuring that children's rights to protection are not just recognised, but realised.

There is ample experience across member states of legal reforms, awareness-raising and public education campaigns to demonstrate how to achieve effective protection. It is clear that the process must be continuing, not one-off, and there must be regular research into and monitoring of children's experiences of violence in their homes and other settings.

Law reform: the essential steps

• Ensuring there are no existing defences, in statute or common law, that justify corporal punishment by parents or others;

• Ensuring that the criminal law on assault applies equally to punitive assaults on children;

• Enacting explicit prohibition of all corporal punishment and all other degrading or humiliating treatment or punishment of children, normally in civil law;

• Providing guidance on appropriate enforcement of these laws, which focuses on protection and promotion of the human rights of children in general and on the best interests of affected children in particular;

• Ensuring comprehensive awareness-raising of the existence of these laws among children, all who live and work with them, and among the general public.

Supporting law reform: educational measures

• Ensuring everyone is aware of the prohibition of all corporal punishment and other inhuman or degrading treatment or humiliation of children, with awareness among children, all who live and work with them and the general public;

• Ensuring comprehensive awareness-raising of children's human rights, including the right to respect for their human dignity and physical integrity;

• Promoting positive, non-violent forms of child-rearing, conflict resolution and education to future parents, parents and other carers, and to the general public;

• Ensuring that children and young people have the opportunity to express their views and participate in planning and actions to eliminate corporal punishment;

• Ensuring that advice and appropriate support is available for all parents and in particular for those who are finding child-rearing stressful;

• Ensuring that children have access to confidential advice and counselling as well as advocacy to challenge violence against them;

• Ensuring effective and appropriate forms of protection for children who may be particularly vulnerable to harmful and humiliating punishment – for example, children with disabilities;

• Ensuring that corporal punishment and other harmful and humiliating forms of discipline of children come within the definition of domestic or family violence and that strategies to eliminate punitive violence against children are built into strategies challenging domestic or family violence;

• Monitoring the effectiveness of abolition by regular research into children's experiences of violence in their homes, schools and other settings, of child protection services and of parents' experiences of and attitudes to violence against children.

Reader's guide

The following abbreviations and short names are used throughout the text:

CRC	Committee on the Rights of the Child (United Nations)
CS-EF	Committee of Experts on Children and Families (Council of Europe)
European Court:	European Court of Human Rights (Council of Europe)
ECHR:	European Convention on Human Rights (full title: Convention for the Protection of Human Rights and Fundamental Freedoms) (Council of Europe)
ECSR	European Committee of Social Rights (Council of Europe)
ENOC	European Network of Ombudspersons for Children (NGO)
NGO	non-governmental organisation
OMCT	World Organisation Against Torture
UNCRC	United Nations Convention on the Rights of the Child

Online appendices: the following appendices, referred to throughout this book, are updated regularly by the Global Initiative to End all Corporal Punishment of Children, to inform on the latest developments concerning corporal punishment in the Council of

Europe member states. They may be accessed at: <http://www.coe.int/children>.

- Appendix 1-online: Progress towards prohibition of corporal punishment in member sates – summary table

- Appendix 2-online: Member states individual reports: law, research and recommendations

- Appendix 3-online: Recommendations to member states by the Committee on the Rights of the Child

- Appendix 4-online: Recommendations to member states by the European Committee of Social Rights

The information on the legal status of the corporal punishment of children in the Council of Europe member states in this text is valid as of June 2007.

1.
Human rights obligations to end all corporal punishment of children

Introduction

Hitting people breaches their fundamental rights to respect for their human dignity and physical integrity. Children are people too – smaller and generally more fragile than adults.

The Council of Europe is based on the principles of respect for the rule of law and enjoyment by all peoples of human rights and fundamental freedoms. Upon ratification of the European Convention on Human Rights (ECHR) and the European Social Charter or revised European Social Charter, the 47 member states of the Council take on binding obligations to respect the human rights of all people within their jurisdictions.

As set out in the following sections, the jurisprudence of the European Court of Human Rights (the European Court) has progressively condemned corporal punishment of children, first in penal systems and schools, and more recently in the home; other decisions have emphasised that banning all corporal punishment does not breach family privacy or religious rights. Case law of the European Social Charter and revised European Social Charter requires all member states to reform their law to prohibit all corporal punishment and other humiliating treatment or punishment of children, and to promote other proactive administrative and educational measures to recognise and realise children's rights to protection. The Council of Europe's Committee of Ministers has condemned corporal punishment and proposed prohibition in a series of recommendations dating back to 1985.[1]

---

1. Committee of Ministers recommendations: "Violence in the family" (R (85) 4), "Social measures concerning violence within the family" (R (90) 2) and "The medico-social aspects of child abuse" (R (93) 2). Committee of Ministers documents are found at <http://www.coe.int/t/cm>.

In addition, all member states of the Council of Europe have ratified the United Nations Convention on the Rights of the Child (UNCRC). This convention includes the obligation to protect children from all forms of physical or mental violence while in the care of parents and others (Article 19). The monitoring body for the UNCRC, the Committee on the Rights of the Child (CRC), consistently interprets the convention as requiring elimination of all corporal punishment. It has recommended prohibition, awareness-raising and public education, to many member states (for all recommendations, see Appendix 3-online), and in June 2006 published a general comment on children's right to protection from corporal punishment and other cruel or degrading forms of punishment (see pp. 37-42).

Other international instruments also demand action against corporal punishment. The UN Universal Declaration of Human Rights (Article 7) and the UN International Covenant on Civil and Political Rights (Article 26) guarantee all people, without any discrimination, equal protection under the law; the Universal Declaration and the International Covenants on Civil and Political Rights and on Economic, Social and Cultural Rights additionally draw special attention to children's rights to special care and protection (Articles 25, 24 and 10 respectively). The UN human rights treaty bodies which monitor compliance with the covenants have condemned corporal punishment of children when examining states' reports.

Although all member states of the Council of Europe have laws prohibiting deliberate assault, in many states these laws do not provide children with the same protection as adults. Some states retain special defences – "reasonable chastisement" or "lawful correction" – for parents and other carers who hit children. In others, while the law on assault appears to apply equally to children, in practice it does not: traditional child-rearing practices, reflected in political and judicial attitudes, condone "disciplinary" assaults. (For summaries of the legal status of corporal punishment in member states, see Appendix 1-online.)

The significance of law reform against corporal punishment of children is that it extends the legal protection that adults take for granted to children. It is ironic that the smallest and most fragile of Europe's citizens should have had to wait until last for this protection.

Box 1 – What is corporal punishment?

The Committee on the Rights of the Child defines corporal or physical punishment as: "any punishment in which physical force is used and intended to cause some degree of pain or discomfort, however light. Most involves hitting ('smacking', 'slapping', 'spanking') children, with the hand or with an implement – a whip, stick, belt, shoe, wooden spoon, etc. But it can also involve, for example, kicking, shaking or throwing children, scratching, pinching, biting, pulling hair or boxing ears, forcing children to stay in uncomfortable positions, burning, scalding or forced ingestion (for example, washing children's mouths out with soap or forcing them to swallow hot spices).

"In the view of the committee, corporal punishment is invariably degrading. In addition, there are other non-physical forms of punishment that are also cruel and degrading and thus incompatible with the convention. These include, for example, punishment which belittles, humiliates, denigrates, scapegoats, threatens, scares or ridicules the child." (General Comment No. 8 (2006) on "The right to protection from corporal punishment and other cruel or degrading forms of punishment", Articles 19; 28, para. 2; and 37, inter alia)

By June 2007, in only 16 member states have explicit bans on all corporal punishment confirmed children's full legal protection (see Chapter 2, pp. 55-66, Appendix 1-online). If children are to enjoy their human rights, these essential legal reforms must be linked with extensive and continuing campaigns to raise awareness of the law and of children's rights to protection, together with education of public and parents to promote positive, non-violent ways of child-rearing and discipline.

Corporal punishment of children within the family remains a hidden issue in many member states; in the few countries where there has been significant interview research with parents and children, it finds shockingly high rates of assault of children of all ages, including babies (see pp. 69-70).

The United Nations global deadline for prohibition

In October 2006 the final report of the UN Secretary General's comprehensive global study on violence against children was submitted to the UN General Assembly. It recommends that states should prohibit all forms of violence, including all corporal punishment, and sets a deadline of 2009 (for details, see pp. 46-49). Welcoming the report, the Council of Europe's Commissioner for Human Rights, Thomas Hammarberg, stated: "Neither tradition, culture, nor the need for discipline can justify or legitimise violence against children ... Europe should be a continent free from corporal punishment. All countries should adopt legislation banning beating and other violence against children in homes as well as in institutions."

Speaking at the launch of the report in New York, Maud de Boer-Buquicchio, Deputy Secretary General of the Council of Europe, stressed "Children's defence against violence is non-negotiable" and emphasised that "children are not mini-persons with mini-rights", stating: "We are ready to play our part for the European region by leading the implementation of the study recommendations there."

The European Convention on Human Rights – developing case law

Successive judgments of the Council of Europe's European Court of Human Rights have found that corporal punishment of children breaches the European Convention on Human Rights (ECHR): first in the 1970s as a sentence of the courts for juvenile offenders; then in schools, including private schools; and most recently within the family home. Decisions and judgments have emphasised the state's duty to protect children wherever they are. Other decisions have confirmed that banning all corporal punishment in the home is a legitimate interference in the family and does not breach parents' or others' rights to respect for family life or religious freedom.

Box 2 – The ECHR and the Court of Human Rights

The Statute of the Council of Europe requires that every member state "must accept the principles of the rule of law and of the enjoyment by all persons within its jurisdiction of human rights and fundamental freedoms" (Article 3, Statute). The drafting of a human rights charter was a high priority for the new Council, established in 1949, and in 1950 the Convention for the Protection of Human Rights and Fundamental Freedoms (referred to as the European Convention on Human Rights) was opened for signature. It entered into force in 1953 and was the first international instrument to protect a broad range of civil and political rights through a treaty that is legally binding on all member states. The Convention established a system of supervision which includes the right of individual victims to challenge breaches of their rights, a system that has been accepted by all member states. Optional Protocols have added to the rights protected by the Convention.

The Court has emphasised that it regards the ECHR as a "living instrument" which "must be interpreted in the light of present-day conditions". In its decisions, the Court increasingly refers to the UN Convention on the Rights of the Child as the standard by which human rights should be realised in the lives of children.

Until 1998, applications alleging breaches of the Convention were examined in a two-stage process, first by the European Commission on Human Rights and then, if the application appeared to reveal a breach and no settlement could be reached between the applicant and the state, generally by the European Court of Human Rights. Since 1998, the process has been unified, with all applications being considered by the Court.

The Committee of Ministers of the Council of Europe supervises governments' execution of judgments of the Court, which are final and binding on the respondent state.[2]

---

2. For a fuller explanation of the ECHR and European Court of Human Rights, see D. Gomien, *Short guide to the European Convention on Human Rights*, 3rd edition, 2005, Council of Europe Publishing.

Judicial corporal punishment of children

The first case concerning corporal punishment to come before the European Court was that of *Tyrer v. UK*. Anthony Tyrer was a 15-year-old citizen of the Isle of Man, a British Crown Dependency, who was sentenced in 1972 to be birched after conviction for assault. The judgment states:

> After waiting in a police station for a considerable time for a doctor to arrive, Mr Tyrer was birched late in the afternoon of the same day. His father and a doctor were present. The applicant was made to take down his trousers and underpants and bend over a table; he was held by two policemen whilst a third administered the punishment, pieces of the birch breaking at the first stroke. The applicant's father lost his self-control and after the third stroke "went for" one of the policemen and had to be restrained.

The Court found that the punishment amounted to degrading punishment in breach of Article 3 of the Convention.[3]

School corporal punishment

By the time the *Tyrer* case came before the Court, two applications concerning school corporal punishment in the United Kingdom had been submitted to the European Commission on Human Rights (until 1998, there was a two-stage process for considering individual applications – see Box 2 above). These applications, by two Scottish mothers, were later combined, and resulted in a 1982 judgment, *Campbell and Cosans v. UK*.[4]

Ms Grace Campbell and Ms Jane Cosans alleged that corporal punishment used in their sons' schools was contrary to Article 3 on protection from inhuman or degrading treatment or punishment. The children were in Scottish schools in which corporal punishment consisted of striking the palm of a child's hand with a leather strap called

---

3. European Court of Human Rights, *Tyrer v. UK*, 1978; all judgments of the Court are available at <http://hudoc.echr.coe.int/>.

4. European Court of Human Rights, *Campbell and Cosans v. UK*, 1982: see note 3.

a tawse. As neither boy had in fact received corporal punishment, this allegation was rejected by the Court.

It did, however, find that the UK had failed to respect the parents' philosophical convictions against the use of corporal punishment. Article 2 of Protocol 1 to the Convention states:

> No person shall be denied the right to education. In the exercise of any functions which it assumes in relation to education and to teaching, the State shall respect the right of parents to ensure such education and teaching in conformity with their own religious and philosophical convictions.

Jeffrey Cosans, aged 15, had been suspended from his school when he refused to accept corporal punishment: the Court found that he had been denied his right to education.

Following this judgment, during the 1980s over 20 other applications concerning school corporal punishment were made by UK schoolchildren and their parents, alleging breaches of their rights under Article 3 (protection from inhuman or degrading punishment) or Article 8 (respect for family and private life) or both. After being declared admissible by the European Commission on Human Rights, in most cases "friendly settlements" were reached, with the UK Government agreeing to make *ex gratia* payments to the families involved.

These successive decisions effectively led to abolition of corporal punishment in all state-supported education in the UK in 1987. But corporal punishment remained legal for pupils in private schools not receiving state support in England and Wales until September 1999, in Scotland until 2000 and in private schools in Northern Ireland until 2003. Some member states had abolished school corporal punishment centuries before: in Poland it was prohibited in 1783.

Parental corporal punishment

In September 1998, the European Court of Human Rights unanimously found that corporal punishment of a young English boy by his stepfather, in the form of repeated hitting with a garden cane, had breached Article 3.[5] Prosecution of the stepfather in a UK court had failed on the ground that the punishment was considered to be "reasonable chastisement". The European Court found the UK was responsible because the domestic law allowing "reasonable chastisement" failed to provide children with adequate protection, including "effective deterrence". The Court ordered the UK to pay £10 000 compensation to the boy. The Court's judgment cites articles of the United Nations Convention on the Rights of the Child, including Article 19 which requires states to protect children from "all forms of physical or mental violence" while in the care of parents and others.

The judgment reveals that when the stepfather was tried in an English court for assault causing actual bodily harm, the judge had advised the jury on the law as follows:

> What is it the prosecution must prove? If a man deliberately and unjustifiably hits another and causes some bodily injury, bruising or swelling, he is guilty of actual bodily harm. What does "unjustifiably" mean in the context of this case? It is a perfectly good defence that the alleged assault was merely the correcting of a child by its parent, in this case the stepfather, provided that the correction be moderate in the manner, the instrument and the quantity of it. Or, put another way, reasonable. It is not for the defendant to prove it was lawful correction. It is for the prosecution to prove it was not.

The jury in the English court acquitted the stepfather of assault.

The execution of judgments of the European Court of Human Rights by the state government concerned is supervised by the Committee of Ministers of the Council of Europe. The Committee is still supervising the execution of *A v. UK* by the UK Government more than eight years after the judgment. At meetings of the Committee, concern has been expressed at the lack of action, including sufficient legislative reform, taken by the UK Government.

---

5. European Court of Human Rights, *A v. UK*, 1998: see note 3.

Abolition of corporal punishment – no breach of family or religious rights

Abolition upholds children's rights and does not breach family or religious rights. In another significant decision in 1982, the European Human Rights Commission declared an application by Swedish parents inadmissible. The parents alleged that the 1979 Swedish ban on parental physical punishment breached their right to respect for family life and to freedom of religion. The parents, belonging to a Protestant free church congregation in Stockholm, believed in the necessity of physical punishment, justifying their beliefs with references to Biblical texts. The Commission concluded that the Swedish law on assault was not unusual or in any way draconian:

> The fact that no distinction is made between the treatment of children by their parents and the same treatment applied to an adult stranger cannot, in the Commission's opinion, constitute "an interference" with respect for the applicant's private and family lives since the consequences of an assault are equated in both cases. ... The Commission finds that the scope of the Swedish law of assault and molestation is a normal measure for the control of violence and that its extension to apply to the ordinary physical chastisement of children by their parents is intended to protect potentially weak and vulnerable members of society.[6]

In a similar decision in September 2000, the European Court rejected unanimously and without a hearing an application by individuals associated with a group of Christian private schools in the UK, who had alleged that the implementation of a ban on corporal punishment in private schools breached parents' rights to freedom of religion and family life.[7]

---

6. European Commission on Human Rights, admissibility decision, *Seven Individuals v. Sweden*, 1982; Application No. 8811/79: see note 3.

7. European Court of Human Rights, decision on admissibility, *Philip Williamson and Others v. UK*, 2000; Application No. 55211/00: see note 3.

The European Committee of Social Rights – monitoring conformity with the European Social Charter

General observations and conclusions

The European Committee of Social Rights (ECSR), monitoring member states' compliance with the European Social Charter and Revised Social Charter, has declared that Article 17 of the Charter requires effective prohibition of all corporal punishment and of any other form of degrading punishment or treatment of children.

Box 3– The European Social Charter

The European Social Charter, which protects fundamental social and economic rights, supplementing the civil and political rights protected by the European Convention on Human Rights, was opened for signature in 1961 and entered into force in 1965. A revised European Social Charter (1996) came into force in 1999 and is gradually replacing the 1961 Charter. States which have ratified the Charter submit reports indicating how they implement the Charter in law and practice. The European Committee of Social Rights determines whether or not national law and practice in the states parties are in conformity with the Charter. Its decisions, known as "conclusions", are published every year.

Under a protocol which came into force in 1998 complaints of violations of the Charter may be lodged with the European Committee of Social Rights (collective complaints procedure). Complaints may be lodged by national and international organisations of employers and trade unions, non-governmental organisations with participative status with the Council of Europe, which are on a list drawn up for this purpose, and, in the case of states which have specifically agreed to this, national non-governmental organisations. By 2007, 14 states had accepted this procedure.

Article 17 of the original Charter requires states to take "all appropriate and necessary measures" to ensure the "effective exercise of the right of mothers and children to social and economic protection". Article 17 of the revised European Social Charter is more detailed and was inspired by the UN Convention on the Rights of the Child. It requires states, among other actions, to take all appropriate and necessary measures "to protect children and young persons against negligence, violence or exploitation".

By January 2007 the committee had found 18 member states – Belgium, Czech Republic, Estonia, France, Greece (where the law changed in 2006; see p. 64), Hungary (where the law changed in 2004; see p. 64), Ireland, Lithuania, Malta, Netherlands (where the law changed in 2007; see p. 65), Poland, Moldova, Romania (where the law changed in 2004; see p. 63), Slovak Republic, Slovenia, Spain, Turkey and the United Kingdom – to be not in conformity with Article 17 because corporal punishment of children is not fully prohibited. See appendices 1- and 2-online for details of the laws in all of these states.

The committee is paying systematic attention to the issue and has deferred conclusions on reports from several other states while awaiting further information (see Appendix 4-online). In 2003, "collective complaints" were registered against five states alleging that they have not prohibited all corporal punishment. In 2004 the ECSR found a violation in three of these cases and the ECSR decisions on the merits of the complaints were made public in May 2005. (See below for more detail.)

Under the reporting procedure, if a state takes no action on an ECSR decision, with the effect that it does not comply with the Charter, the Committee of Ministers may address a recommendation to that state, asking it to change the situation in law and/or practice. The Committee of Ministers' work is prepared by an intergovernmental committee comprising government representatives of the states parties to the Charter, assisted by observers from European trade unions and employers' organisations.

Under the collective complaints mechanism, the committee decides whether a complaint is admissible and, if so, takes a decision on the merits of the complaint, which it forwards to the parties concerned and to the Committee of Ministers in a report, which is made public within four months of being forwarded. The Committee of Ministers adopts a resolution, if appropriate, and may recommend that the state concerned take specific measures to bring the situation into line with the Charter.

A 2001 European Committee of Social Rights general observation concludes:

> that Article 17 requires a prohibition in legislation against any form of violence against children, whether at school, in other institutions, in their home or elsewhere. [The committee] furthermore considers that any other form of degrading punishment or treatment of children must be prohibited in legislation and combined with adequate sanctions in penal or civil law.[8]

The observation states: "The committee does not find it acceptable that a society which prohibits any form of physical violence between adults would accept that adults subject children to physical violence." (See Appendix III for an extract of the general observation.)

Since issuing its general observation, the committee has systematically asked member states to provide information on the legality of corporal punishment of children in the home, in schools and other institutions and all forms of care. In some cases, the committee has deferred issuing a conclusion on compliance with Article 17 until it receives information on the legality of corporal punishment (for example, Bulgaria and Luxembourg).

In February 2003 the committee issued a finding of non-conformity with Article 17, for the first time on the grounds that a member state – Poland – had not prohibited corporal punishment in the family. The committee examined Poland's report on implementation of Article 17 and concluded:

> Ministerial regulations prohibit the corporal punishment of children in public schools. The committee requests information about the situation in private schools and in institutions; it notes that the corporal punish-

---

8. European Committee of Social Rights, General observations regarding Articles 7 (para. 10) and 17, *Conclusions XV-2*, Vol. 1, General Introduction, p. 26.

ment of children in the home is not prohibited. Therefore, the situation is not in conformity with the Charter in this respect ... The committee concludes that the situation in Poland is not in conformity with Article 17 of the Charter on the following grounds: corporal punishment of children in the home is not prohibited.[9]

Since finding Poland not to be in conformity with Article 17, similar conclusions were issued in 2003 on reports from France, Romania, Slovak Republic and Slovenia. In its conclusions on France, the committee states:

As regards corporal punishment of children, the committee notes that according to the report corporal punishment of children is not explicitly prohibited in the home, in school or in other institutions. Although the Penal Code prohibits violence against the person and provides for increased penalties where the victim is under 15 years of age or where the perpetrator is related to the child or has authority over the child, the committee notes that these provisions of the Penal Code do not necessarily cover all forms of corporal punishment and therefore finds that the situation is not in conformity with the revised Charter.[10]

States' compliance with Article 17 was examined by the ECSR during 2004. In its conclusions (2005), it found a number of states were not in conformity with Article 17 of the Charter because of the absence of prohibition in law of corporal punishment within the family, or in some cases other settings (Belgium, Czech Republic, Estonia, France, Greece, Hungary, Lithuania, Malta, Netherlands, Poland, Moldova, Romania, Slovenia, Spain, Turkey and United Kingdom). (Hungary, Romania, Greece and Netherlands have since prohibited all corporal punishment, and Lithuania, Luxembourg, Portugal, Slovak Republic, Slovenia and Spain are committed to legal reform (appendices 1- and 2-online)).

---

9. European Committee of Social Rights, *Conclusions XVI-2*, Vol. 2, Chapter 14.
10. European Committee of Social Rights, *Conclusions 2003*, Vol. 1, pp. 185, 187.

For example, on Czech Republic, the committee concluded:

> The report states that under the amended Families Act (1998), parents have the right to use reasonable correctional means that do not affect the child's dignity nor endanger the child's health, or his physical, emotional, intellectual, and moral development. The committee notes that this provision does not explicitly prohibit the corporal punishment of children within the family. It notes from another source that there is no legislation explicitly prohibiting corporal punishment, and that it is practised in the family, in schools and in other public institutions, including alternative care contexts. The committee therefore considers that since there is no explicit prohibition in legislation of corporal punishment in the home, in schools and in other institutions, the situation cannot be considered to be in conformity with Article 17 of the Charter on this point.[11]

The Committee noted a lack of progress by France and Poland since 2003, and in 2005 reiterated its earlier findings of non-conformity. On France, it stated:

> In the previous conclusion the committee noted that the Penal Code prohibits violence against the person and provides for increased penalties where the victim is under 15 years of age or where the perpetrator is related to the child or has authority over the child, but does not necessarily cover all forms of corporal punishment which it found not to be in conformity with the Revised Charter. The committee finds no information in the report that the situation has changed. The committee notes therefore that corporal punishment is not prohibited in the home or in institutions and other childcare settings and that this situation is not in conformity with the Revised Charter.[12]

In its conclusions on Belgium and Greece, the committee referred to its decisions on the merits in the complaints brought against these states by the World Organisation against Torture (OMCT) under

---

11. European Committee of Social Rights, *Conclusions XVII-2*, July 2005.
12. Ibid., March 2005.

the collective complaints procedure (see below). For example, on Belgium:

> the committee recalls its decision on the merits in *World Organisation against Torture (OMCT) v. Belgium* (Collective Complaint No. 21/2003, decision on the merits, 7 December 2004), in which it found that Belgium was in violation of Article 17 of the Charter since there was no prohibition in legislation of corporal punishment of children within the family. The committee notes that the situation has not been remedied .... The committee concludes that the situation in Belgium is not in conformity with Article 17 of the Charter on the ground that there is no prohibition in legislation of all corporal punishment of children within the family.[13]

Extracts from all the conclusions of the European Committee of Social Rights relating to corporal punishment are reproduced at Appendix 4-online.

Collective complaints

In December 2003, collective complaints were declared admissible against five countries – Belgium, Greece, Ireland, Italy and Portugal – alleging that they were not in conformity with the Charters because all corporal punishment and other humiliating treatment of children was not prohibited.[14] A decision on these cases was reached by the ECSR in December 2004. The committee found a violation of Article 17 in three of the complaints.

In *World Organisation Against Torture (OMCT) v. Greece* Collective Complaint No. 17/2003 the committee found that there was a breach of Article 17 on the grounds that corporal punishment was not adequately prohibited in the home, in secondary schools and in institutions caring for children. It highlighted that, even if violence against the person is punished under criminal law provisions and subject to

---

13. Ibid., July 2005.

14. These five collective complaints are referred to as follows: No. 17/2003 *OMCT v. Greece*, No. 18/2003 *OMCT v. Ireland*, No. 19/2003 *OMCT v. Italy*, No. 20/2003 *OMCT v. Portugal* and No. 21/2003 *OMCT v. Belgium*. Details on the consideration and the progress of these complaints can be found at <http://www.coe.int/T/E/Human _ Rights/Esc>.

increased penalties where the victim is a child, this does not constitute sufficient prohibition to comply with Article 17.1 of the Revised
Charter. The committee found that the legal provisions relied upon
by the Greek Government did not constitute an adequate legal basis.
Since the decision of the committee, Greece has introduced legislation prohibiting corporal punishment in all settings.

In *OMCT v. Belgium* Collective Complaint No. 21/2003, the committee reached a similar decision: it found the law did not adequately
prohibit all forms of violence, including corporal punishment by parents and "other persons", including educational purposes, and so the
situation in Belgium was in violation of Article 17 of the Charter.

Likewise the committee found Ireland to be in violation of Article
17, in *OMCT v. Ireland* Collective Complaint No. 18/2003. The committee noted in the decision that corporal punishment of children
within the home is permitted in Ireland by virtue of the existence of
the common law defence of "reasonable chastisement", although the
criminal law will protect children from very serious forms of violence.
As regards the situation of children in foster care, residential care and
certain childminding settings, the committee noted the existence of
guidelines, standards and inspections etc., but noted that these did
not have the force of law and therefore the common-law defence of
"reasonable chastisement" remained *prima facie* applicable.

The committee found that there was no violation of Article 17 in
the cases of *OMCT v. Italy* Collective Complaint No. 19/2003 and
OMCT v. Portugal Collective complaint No. 20/2003. On the situation in Italy, the committee noted that the law (both criminal and
civil) as interpreted by the courts adequately prohibited all forms of
violence regardless of where it occurs or of the identity of the alleged
perpetrator. Similarly, the committee noted that the law in Portugal
as interpreted by the Supreme Court was sufficient. It stated in its
Decision on the merits:

> according to a series of Supreme Court decisions even a simple slap
> causing no bodily injury is considered as a corporal assault falling into

the scope of Section 143 ... Given Section 143 of the Criminal Code as interpreted by the Supreme Court, the committee holds that in Portugal the prohibition of all forms of violence has a legislative basis; it has the potential to reach all forms of violence regardless of where it occurs or to the identity of the alleged perpetrator; and it is backed by adequate, dissuasive and proportionate sanctions.[15]

But in April 2006, the Supreme Court in Portugal, in a case concerning cruelty and ill-treatment of mentally disabled children in a children's institution, ruled that slaps and spankings are "legal" and "acceptable" in child-rearing, and that failure to use these methods of punishment could even amount to "educational neglect". In May 2006, the OMCT submitted a second complaint alleging that domestic law in Portugal does not explicitly nor effectively prohibit all corporal punishment of children (*OMCT v. Portugal* Collective Complaint No. 34/2006). On 5 April 2007, the ECSR agreed unanimously with the complainant and concluded that Portugal was in violation of Article 17.

The Committee of Ministers – recommendations to end corporal punishment

The Committee of Ministers of the Council of Europe first condemned corporal punishment of children in Recommendation No. R (85) 4 on violence in the family, adopted in 1985. The preamble states that: the defence of the family involves the protection of all its members against any form of violence, which all too often occurs among them. Violence affects: in particular children on the one side and women on the other, though in differing ways and children are entitled to special protection by society against any form of discrimination or oppression and against any abuse of authority in the family and other institutions". The recommendation proposes that states review their legislation on the power to punish children in order to limit or indeed

---

15. Decision on the merits of Collective Complaint No. 20/2003 World Organisation against Torture (OMCT) v. Portugal (paras 38 and 42): see note 14.

prohibit corporal punishment, even if violation of such a prohibition does not necessarily entail a criminal penalty.

The recommendation's explanatory memorandum describes corporal punishment as an "evil which must at least be discouraged as a first step towards outright prohibition. It is the very assumption that corporal punishment of children is legitimate that opens the way to all kinds of excesses and makes the traces and symptoms of such punishment acceptable to third parties".

In a 1990 recommendation to member states on "Social measures concerning violence within the family",[16] the Committee notes that "trends towards the democratisation of the family, implying respect for members of the family as individuals with equal rights and equal opportunities, can help to discourage violence". Under "Measures for children", the recommendation states: "The general condemnation of corporal punishment and other forms of degrading treatment as a means of education, and of the need for violence-free education, should be emphasised."

In 1993, in Recommendation R (93) 2 on "the medico-social aspects of child abuse", the Committee of Ministers, noting the United Nations Convention on the Rights of the Child, urged member states "to emphasise the rights of all children and young people to freedom from abuse and the need to change patterns of upbringing and behaviour which threaten this" and "to minimise levels of violence within society and the resort to violence in child-rearing practices". In 2006, the Committee of Ministers issued a recommendation calling for non-violent positive parenting[17] in the context of respect for and the implementation of children's rights.

In April 2006, the Council of Europe launched the programme, "Building a Europe for and with Children", aiming to combat all

---

16. Committee of Ministers recommendations: "Violence in the family" (R (85) 4) and "Social measures concerning violence within the family" (R (90) 2), see note 1.

17. Committee of Ministers Rec(2006)19 on policy to support positive parenting: see note 1.

forms of violence against children. The Committee of Ministers commented:

> Given that the member states of the Council of Europe have entered into numerous commitments under general human rights conventions and specific conventions on children's rights and that human rights treaties of the Council of Europe (as well as the UN Convention on the Rights of the Child) require states to prohibit and fight all forms of violence and ill-treatment of children, the programme will assist member states in fulfilling their obligations under such treaties. It will be done in particular by implementing integrated prevention policies and alerting professional circles and the general public to the problem. The programme will address all forms of violence, wherever it takes place (family, school, resident institutions, the community, media and cyberspace) with special attention to fighting sexual abuse and corporal punishment.[18]

The United Nations Convention on the Rights of the Child and its monitoring body the Committee on the Rights of the Child

The United Nations Convention on the Rights of the Child (UNCRC) was adopted by the UN General Assembly in 1989. As at 2007, the convention had been ratified by 193 states, including all member states of the Council of Europe. Its status as the most ratified international human rights treaty enhances the authority of its detailed principles and standards.

The UNCRC is the first treaty to address directly the protection of children from violence. Article 19 of the convention requires states to take:

> all appropriate legislative, administrative, social and educational measures to protect the child from all forms of physical or mental violence, injury or abuse, neglect or negligent treatment, maltreatment or exploitation including sexual abuse, while in the care of parent(s), legal guardian(s) or any other person who has the care of the child.

---

18. Reply of the Committee of Ministers to Written Question No. 492, 29 September 2006: see note 1.

The Committee on the Rights of the Child (CRC), the internationally elected treaty body, which monitors implementation by examining reports from ratifying states, has identified four articles as providing general principles:

- Article 2: non-discrimination – all UNCRC rights must be respected and ensured for each child within a state's jurisdiction without discrimination of any kind;

- Article 3: the best interests of the child must be a primary consideration in all actions concerning children;

- Article 6: the right to life and maximum development – states must ensure "to the maximum extent possible the survival and development of the child";

- Article 12: states must assure the child's right to express their views freely on all matters concerning them and to have those views given due weight in accordance with age and maturity.

The convention upholds the family as "the natural environment for the growth and well-being of all its members and particularly children" (preamble), promotes recognition of parents' common responsibilities for the upbringing and development of the child, with the child's best interests as their basic concern, and the state's obligation to support parents (Article 18). It emphasises states' undertaking to provide the child with "such protection and care as is necessary for his or her well-being", taking account of the responsibilities of parents and others legally responsible (Article 3.2).

In relation to education, the convention requires states to ensure that school discipline is administered "in a manner consistent with the child's human dignity and in conformity with the present convention" (Article 28.2). Article 37 requires states to ensure that "no child shall be subjected to torture or other cruel, inhuman or degrading treatment or punishment". Under Article 40, all children involved with juvenile justice systems have the right "to be treated in a manner consistent with the promotion of the child's sense of dignity and worth".

The Committee on the Rights of the Child has consistently inter-preted the convention as requiring the prohibition of all corporal punishment of children, including within the family home. In June 2006, the committee adopted General Comment No. 8[19] on children's right to protection from corporal punishment, which re-emphasised its condemnation of all forms of corporal punishment of children and the obligation on state parties to prohibit and eliminate it through legislative, administrative and other awareness-raising and educa-tional measures (see below).

The CRC's general comments on corporal punishment

General Comment No. 8 on "The right to protection from corpo-ral punishment and other cruel or degrading forms of punishment (Articles 19; 28, para. 2; and 37, inter alia)", adopted by the CRC at its 42nd session in Geneva in May/June 2006, aims: "to highlight the obligation of all states parties to move quickly to prohibit and elimi-nate all corporal punishment and all other cruel or degrading forms of punishment of children and to outline the legislative and other awareness-raising and educational measures that states must take (para. 2)". As well as being an obligation of states parties under the Convention on the Rights of the Child, addressing and eliminating corporal punishment of children is "a key strategy for reducing and preventing all forms of violence in societies (para. 3).

In paragraph 11 of its general comment, the committee defines cor-poral or physical punishment:

> as any punishment in which physical force is used and intended to cause some degree of pain or discomfort, however light. Most involves hitting ("smacking", "slapping", "spanking") children, with the hand or with an implement – whip, stick, belt, shoe, wooden spoon, etc. But it can also

---

19. General Comment No. 8 is found at <www.ohchr.org/english/bodies/crc/comments htm>.

involve, for example, kicking, shaking or throwing children, scratching, pinching, burning, scalding or forced ingestion (for example, washing children's mouths out with soap or forcing them to swallow hot spices). In the view of the committee, corporal punishment is invariably degrading. In addition, there are other non-physical forms of punishment which are also cruel and degrading, and thus incompatible with the convention. These include, for example, punishment which belittles, humiliates, denigrates, scapegoats, threatens, scares or ridicules the child.

Children are subjected to such punishment in all settings and it must be addressed and eliminated in all settings, including within the home and family.

The committee distinguishes between violence and humiliation as forms of punishment, which it rejects, and discipline of children in the form of "necessary guidance and direction", which is essential for healthy growth of children. The committee also differentiates between punitive physical actions against children and physical interventions aimed at protecting children from harm.

Human rights standards

The basis of the human rights obligation to prohibit and eliminate all corporal punishment and all other degrading forms of punishment lies in the right of every person to respect for his/her dignity and physical integrity, and equal protection under the law. The committee traces this back to the original International Bill of Human Rights – "The dignity of each and every individual is the fundamental guiding principle of international human rights law" (para. 16) – and shows how the Convention on the Rights of the Child builds on these principles. Quoting Article 19 of the convention, which requires states to protect children "from all forms of physical or mental violence", the committee states (para. 18):

> There is no ambiguity: "all forms of physical or mental violence" does not leave room for any level of legalised violence against children. Corporal punishment and other cruel or degrading forms of punishment are forms of violence and the state must take all appropriate legislative, administrative, social and educational measures to eliminate them.

The fact that Articles 19 and (on school discipline) 28 do not specifically refer to corporal punishment in no way undermines the obligation to prohibit and eliminate it (paras. 20-22):

> [T]he convention, like all human rights instruments, must be regarded as a living instrument, whose interpretation develops over time. In the 17 years since the convention was adopted, the prevalence of corporal punishment of children in their homes, schools and other institutions has become more visible, through the reporting process under the convention and through research and advocacy by, among others, national human rights institutions and non-governmental organisations (NGOs).

> Once visible, it is clear that the practice directly conflicts with the equal and inalienable rights of children to respect for their human dignity and physical integrity. The distinct nature of children, their initial dependent and developmental state, their unique human potential as well as their vulnerability, all demand the need for more, rather than less, legal and other protection from all forms of violence.

> The committee emphasises that eliminating violent and humiliating punishment of children, through law reform and other necessary measures, is an immediate and unqualified obligation of states parties.

The committee goes on to note that this approach is mirrored in the work of other human rights treaty monitoring bodies and regional human rights mechanisms, including the European Court of Human Rights, the Inter-American Court of Human Rights and the African Commission on Human and Peoples' Rights.

Answering common arguments

Common arguments by governments against prohibition of all corporal punishment are also addressed by the committee. For example, in response to the contention that a certain degree of "reasonable" or "moderate" corporal punishment is in the "best interests" of the child, the committee states that (para. 26):

> interpretation of a child's best interests must be consistent with the whole convention, including the obligation to protect children from all

forms of violence and the requirement to give due weight to the child's views; it cannot be used to justify practices, including corporal punishment and other forms of cruel or degrading punishment, which conflict with the child's human dignity and right to physical integrity".

And there is no conflict between realising children's rights and the importance of the family unit, which the convention fully upholds. The committee recognises that some people justify the use of corporal punishment through religious faith teachings and texts, but it again notes that "practice of a religion or belief must be consistent with respect for others' human dignity and physical integrity" and "[f]reedom to practise one's religion or belief may be legitimately limited in order to protect the fundamental rights and freedoms of others" (para. 29).

Legal reform

Legal reform is essential in eliminating corporal punishment. All provisions that allow a "reasonable" degree of corporal punishment – whether in statute or in case/common law – should be repealed, as should all legislation specifically regulating administration of corporal punishment, for example in schools or other institutions. But the law must also explicitly prohibit corporal punishment in all settings, as the committee explains (para. 34):

> In the light of the traditional acceptance of violent and humiliating forms of punishment of children, a growing number of states have recognised that simply repealing authorisation of corporal punishment and any existing defences is not enough. In addition, explicit prohibition of corporal punishment and other cruel or degrading forms of punishment, in their civil or criminal legislation, is required in order to make it absolutely clear that it is as unlawful to hit or "smack" or "spank" a child as to do so to an adult, and that the criminal law on assault does apply equally to such violence, regardless whether it is termed discipline or "reasonable correction".

Other measures and mechanisms required

The committee expects more than legal reform (para. 35):

> Once the criminal law applies fully to assaults on children, the child is protected from corporal punishment wherever they are and whoever is the perpetrator. But in the view of the committee, given the traditional acceptance of corporal punishment, it is essential that the applicable sectoral legislation – e.g. family law, education law, law relating to all forms of alternative care and justice systems, employment law – clearly prohibits its use in the relevant settings. In addition, it is valuable if professional codes of ethics and guidance for teachers, carers and others and also the rules or charters of institutions emphasise the illegality of corporal punishment and other cruel or degrading forms of punishment.

The committee emphasises that law reform should be accompanied by awareness-raising, guidance and training, because the primary purpose of such reform is prevention – "to prevent violence against children by changing attitudes and practice, underlining children's right to equal protection and providing an unambiguous foundation for child protection and for the promotion of positive, non-violent and participatory forms of child-rearing" (para. 38). Prohibition in law does not mean that all cases of corporal punishment of children by parents should lead to prosecution (para. 40): "[w]hile all reports of violence against children should be appropriately investigated and their protection from significant harm assured, the aim should be to stop parents using violent or other cruel or degrading punishment through supportive and educational, not punitive, interventions".

Effective prohibition requires "comprehensive awareness-raising of children's right to protection and of the laws which reflect this right" (para. 45) and the consistent promotion of positive, non-violent relationships and education "to parents, carers, teachers and all others who work with children and families" (para. 46). While the convention does not prescribe in detail how parenting should be carried out, it does "provide a framework of principles to guide relationships both within the family and between teachers, carers and others and children" (para. 46). For example, children's developmental needs must be respected, their best interests are fundamental, and their views should be given due weight.

Finally, states parties should monitor their progress in eliminating corporal punishment and other cruel or degrading forms of punishment; they should use interview research with children, establish independent monitoring bodies and report on all measures taken in their periodic state party reports to the committee.

The development of the CRC's views

In 2000 and 2001, before adopting General Comment No. 8, the committee held two days of general discussion on violence against children. After the second, in September 2001, focusing on violence in the family and schools, its recommendations included:

> The committee urges states parties to enact or repeal, as a matter of urgency, their legislation in order to prohibit all forms of violence, however light, within the family and in schools, including as a form of discipline, as required by the provisions of the convention and in particular Articles 19, 28 and 37(a) and taking into account Articles 2, 3, 6 and 12 as well as 4, 5, 9, 18, 24, 27, 29 and 39.

In 2001 the committee adopted its first general comment, on the Aims of Education (Article 29.1 of the UNCRC), which states (para. 7):

> Children do not lose their human rights by virtue of passing through the school gates. Thus, for example, education must be provided in a way that respects the inherent dignity of the child, enables the child to express his or her views freely in accordance with Article 12(1) and to participate in school life. Education must also be provided in a way that respects the strict limits on discipline reflected in Article 28(2) and promotes non-violence in school. The committee has repeatedly made clear in its concluding observations that the use of corporal punishment does not respect the inherent dignity of the child nor the strict limits on school discipline. Compliance with the values recognised in

Article 29(1) clearly requires that schools be child-friendly in the fullest sense of that term and that they be consistent in all respects with the dignity of the child.

The committee started to examine reports from states parties to the UNCRC in 1993. From early on, it showed particular concern at persisting legal and social acceptance of corporal punishment of children, in their homes, schools, other institutions and penal systems. It consistently stated that corporal punishment of children, within the family or in any other setting, is not compatible with the convention. In concluding observations on over 130 states, in all continents, the committee has recommended prohibition of all corporal punishment, with education campaigns to encourage positive, non-violent child-rearing and education.[20] (See Appendix 3-online for CRC recommendations to Council of Europe member states.)

In examining states parties' reports, the committee has particularly criticised laws, existing in many countries, that allow some level of violent punishment – "reasonable chastisement", "moderate correction" and so on. Examining Spain's first report under the UNCRC, it expressed concern "at the wording of Article 154 of the Spanish Civil Code which provides that parents 'may administer punishment to their children reasonably and in moderation', which may be interpreted to allow for actions in contradiction with Article 19 of the Convention". It recommended revision to bring the law "into full conformity with Article 19".[21] Examining Spain's second report, the committee said it "deeply regrets" the law had not yet been revised.

---

20. Committee on the Rights of the Child: documents, including its concluding observations on states parties' reports under the UN Convention on the Rights of the Child, are available at <http://www.unhchr.ch/html/menu2/6/crc/>. The website of the Global Initiative to End All Corporal Punishment of Children includes the text of all the CRC's recommendations on corporal punishment, analysed by session and by state: <http://www.endcorporalpunishment.org>.

21. Committee on the Rights of the Child, concluding observations on Spain's Initial Report under the Convention on the Rights of the Child, 24 October 1994, CRC/C/15/Add.28, paras. 10 and 18: see note 20.

The committee reiterates its previous recommendation to amend Article 154 in order to delete the reference to reasonable chastisement. It further recommends that the state party:

• Prohibit all forms of violence, including corporal punishment, in the upbringing of children, in conformity with Article 19 of the convention;

• Conduct awareness campaigns and promote alternative forms of discipline in families.[22]

Similarly, when the committee examined the UK's report in 1995, it expressed concern about:

the national legal provisions dealing with reasonable chastisement within the family. The imprecise nature of the expression of reasonable chastisement as contained in these legal provisions may pave the way for it to be interpreted in a subjective and arbitrary manner. Thus, the committee is concerned that legislative and other measures relating to the physical integrity of children do not appear to be compatible with the provisions and principles of the convention, including those of its Articles 3, 19 and 37. The committee is equally concerned that privately funded and managed schools are still permitted to administer corporal punishment to children in attendance there, which does not appear to be compatible with the provisions of the convention, including those of its Article 28, paragraph 2.

The committee went on to recommend:

that physical punishment of children in families be prohibited in the light of the provisions set out in Articles 3 and 19 of the convention. In connection with the child's right to physical integrity, as recognised by the convention, namely in its Articles 19, 28, 29 and 37, and in the light of the best interests of the child, the committee suggests that the state party consider the possibility of undertaking additional education campaigns. Such measures would help to change societal attitudes towards

---

22. Committee on the Rights of the Child, concluding observations on Spain's Second Report under the Convention on the Rights of the Child, 13 June 2002, CRC/C/15/Add.185, paras. 30 and 31a, b: see note 20.

the use of physical punishment in the family and foster the acceptance of the legal prohibition of the physical punishment of children.

The committee also recommended prohibition of corporal punishment in all private schools.[23]

In 2002 the committee adopted its conclusions on the UK's second report:

> The committee welcomes the abolition of corporal punishment in all schools in England, Wales and Scotland following its 1995 recommendations (ibid., para. 32) but is concerned that this abolition has not yet been extended to cover all private schools in Northern Ireland. It welcomes the adoption by the National Assembly for Wales of regulations prohibiting corporal punishment in all forms of day care, including childminding, but is very concerned that legislation prohibiting all corporal punishment in this context is not yet in place in England, Scotland or Northern Ireland.
>
> In light of its previous recommendation, the committee deeply regrets that the state party persists in retaining the defence of "reasonable chastisement" and has taken no significant action towards prohibiting all corporal punishment of children in the family.
>
> The committee is of the opinion that the Government's proposals to limit rather than to remove the "reasonable chastisement" defence do not comply with the principles and provisions of the convention and the aforementioned recommendations, particularly since they constitute a serious violation of the dignity of the child (see similar observations of the Committee on Economic, Social and Cultural Rights, E/C.12/1/ Add.79, para. 36). Moreover, they suggest that some forms of corporal punishment are acceptable, thereby undermining educational measures to promote positive and non-violent discipline.

---

23. Committee on the Rights of the Child, concluding observations on the UK's Initial Report under the Convention on the Rights of the Child, 15 February 1995, CRC/C/15/Add.34, paras. 16, 31 and 32: see note 20.

The committee recommends that the state party:

• With urgency adopt legislation throughout the state party to remove the "reasonable chastisement" defence and prohibit all corporal punishment in the family and in any other contexts not covered by existing legislation;

• Promote positive, participatory and non-violent forms of discipline and respect for children's equal right to human dignity and physical integrity, involving children and parents and all those who work with and for them, and carry out public education programmes on the negative consequences of corporal punishment.[24]

The committee has made similar recommendations to almost all member states of the Council of Europe (see Appendix 3-online). Where countries have prohibited all corporal punishment, the committee has congratulated them.

The United Nations Secretary-General's study on violence against children

In 2001, on the recommendation of the Committee on the Rights of the Child, the United Nations general assembly in its resolution 56/138 requested the UN secretary general to conduct an in-depth study on the question of violence against children and to put forward recommendations for consideration by member states for appropriate action. In February 2003, Paulo Sérgio Pinheiro was appointed by the secretary general as the independent expert to lead this study, the first comprehensive global study on violence against children.

During 2005, nine regional consultations were held in connection with the study in all parts of the world. Recommendations developed

---

24. Committee on the Rights of the Child, concluding observations on the UK's Second Report under the Convention on the Rights of the Child, 9 October 2002, CRC/C/15/Add.188, paras. 35-37, 38a, b: see note 20.

at every consultation included calls for the prohibition and elimination of all corporal punishment.

Professor Pinheiro notes in the study report[25] that violence against children exists in every country of the world, cutting across culture, class, education, income and ethnic origin (Introduction, paras. 1-2):

> In every region, in contradiction to human rights obligations and children's developmental needs, violence against children is socially approved, and is frequently legal and state-authorised.

> The study should mark a turning point – an end to adult justification of violence against children, whether accepted as "tradition" or disguised as "discipline". There can be no compromise in challenging violence against children. Children's uniqueness – their potential and vulnerability, their dependence on adults – makes it imperative that they have more, not less, protection from violence.

The report recommends prohibition of all forms of violence against children, in all settings, including all corporal punishment and all other cruel, inhuman or degrading forms of punishment, drawing the attention of states to the CRC's General Comment No. 8 (see p. 37). The report calls for prohibition of all violence against children to be completed by 2009 (para. 116). It also recommends that states and civil society should strive to transform attitudes that condone or normalise violence against children, including stereo-typical gender roles and discrimination, acceptance of corporal punishment and harmful traditional practices. States should ensure that children's rights are known and understood, including by children. Public information campaigns should be used to sensitise the public about the harmful effects that violence has on children.

---

25. The report submitted to the general assembly is found at <http://www.violencestudy.org/IMG/pdf/English.pdf>. For further information on the study, and text of the complementary *World report on violence against children*, see <http://www.violencestudy.org/r25>.

The study considers violence against children in the various settings in which it occurs, starting with the home and family (paras. 41 and 42):

> Violence against children in the family may frequently take place in the context of discipline and takes the form of physical, cruel or humiliating punishment. Harsh treatment and punishment in the family are common in both industrialised and developing countries. Children, as reported in studies and speaking for themselves during the Study's regional consultations, highlighted the physical and psychological hurt they suffer as a result of these forms of treatment and proposed positive and effective alternative forms of discipline.

> Physical violence is often accompanied by psychological violence. Insults, name-calling, isolation, rejection, threats, emotional indifference and belittling are all forms of violence that can be detrimental to a child's psychological development and well-being – especially when it comes from a respected adult such as a parent. It is of critical importance that parents be encouraged to employ exclusively non-violent methods of discipline.

Introducing the detailed recommendations in the report, Professor Pinheiro notes that UN member states have already made commitments to protect children from all forms of violence (para. 91):

> However, we must accept – from children's testimony during the study process, as well as reflected in research, that these commitments are far from being fulfilled. The core message of the study is that no violence against children is justifiable; all violence against children is preventable. There should be no more excuses. Member states must act now with urgency to fulfil their human rights obligations and other commitments to ensure protection from all forms of violence. While legal obligations lie with states, all sectors of society, all individuals, share the responsibility of condemning and preventing violence against children and responding to child victims. None of us can look children in the eye, if we continue to approve or condone any form of violence against them.

Extracts from the report's recommendations

The following are extracts from paragraphs 98, 100 and 110 of the above-mentioned report.

> Prohibit all violence against children: ... I urge states to prohibit all forms of violence against children, in all settings, including all corporal punishment ... and other cruel, inhuman or degrading treatment or punishment, as required by international treaties, including the Convention against Torture and Other Cruel, Inhuman or Degrading Treatment or Punishment and the Convention on the Rights of the Child. I draw attention to General Comment No. 8 (2006) of the Committee on the Rights of the Child on the right of the child to protection from corporal punishment and other cruel or degrading forms of punishment (Articles 19, 28, para. 2, and 37, inter alia) (CRC/C/GC/8).

> Promote non-violent values and awareness-raising: I recommend that states and civil society should strive to transform attitudes that condone or normalise violence against children, including stereotypical gender roles and discrimination, acceptance of corporal punishment and harmful traditional practices. States should ensure that children's rights are disseminated and understood, including by children. Public information campaigns should be used to sensitise the public about the harmful effects that violence has on children. States should encourage the media to promote non-violent values and implement guidelines to ensure full respect for the rights of the child in all media coverage.

One of the "setting-specific recommendations" is that, in the home and family, member states should:

> develop gender-sensitive parent education programmes focusing on non-violent forms of discipline. Such programmes should promote healthy parent-child relationships and orient parents towards constructive and positive forms of discipline and child development approaches, taking into account children's evolving capacities and the importance of respecting their views.

Other international human rights instruments and their monitoring mechanisms

The Human Rights Committee

The Human Rights Committee monitors the implementation of the United Nations International Covenant on Civil and Political Rights. In a general comment adopted in 1992 on Article 7 of the covenant ("No one shall be subjected to torture or to cruel, inhuman or degrading treatment or punishment") the committee states:

> The prohibition in Article 7 relates not only to acts that cause physical pain but also to acts that cause mental suffering to the victim. In the committee's view, moreover, the prohibition must extend to corporal punishment, including excessive chastisement ordered as a punishment for a crime or as an educative or disciplinary measure. It is appropriate to emphasise in this regard that Article 7 protects, in particular, children, pupils and patients in teaching and medical institutions.[26]

In examining states' reports, the committee has expressed concern about the use of corporal punishment and recommended its prohibition in the family, schools and penal systems.[27]

The Committee on Economic, Social and Cultural Rights

In 1999 the Committee on Economic, Social and Cultural Rights, which oversees the implementation of the United Nations International Covenant on Economic, Social and Cultural Rights, adopted a general comment on "The Right to Education".[28] It states:

---

26. Human Rights Committee, General Comment No. 20 on Article 7 of the International Covenant on Civil and Political Rights, HRI/GEN/1/Rev.4, p. 108; this general comment replaced the committee's 1982 General Comment No. 7 on Article 7. All Human Rights Committee documents are online at <http://www.unhchr.ch/html/menu2/6/hrc.htm>.

27. For example, see concluding observations on Ireland's Second Report, A/55/40, paras. 422-451, para. 8, 24 July 2000; concluding observations on Poland's Fourth Report, CCPR/C/79/Add.110, para. 25, 29 July 1999; concluding observations on UK's Fourth Report, CCPR/C/79/Add.55, para. 8, 27 July 1995.

28. Committee on Economic, Social and Cultural Rights, General Comment No. 11 on "The right to education", 1999, HRI/GEN/1/Rev.5, p. 83. All the committee's documents are online at <http://www.unhchr.ch/html/menu2/6/cescr.htm>.

In the committee's view, corporal punishment is inconsistent with the fundamental guiding principle of international human rights law enshrined in the Preambles to the Universal Declaration of Human Rights and both Covenants: the dignity of the individual. Other aspects of school discipline may also be inconsistent with human dignity, such as public humiliation. Nor should any form of discipline breach other rights under the Covenant, such as the right to food. A state party is required to take measures to ensure that discipline which is inconsistent with the Covenant does not occur in any public or private educational institution within its jurisdiction. The committee welcomes initiatives taken by some state parties which actively encourage schools to introduce "positive", non-violent approaches to school discipline.

A footnote states:

In formulating this paragraph, the committee has taken note of the practice evolving elsewhere in the international human rights system, such as the interpretation given by the Committee on the Rights of the Child to Article 28(2) of the Convention on the Rights of the Child, as well as the Human Rights Committee's interpretation of Article 7 of the International Covenant on Civil and Political Rights.

In 2002, the committee advocated the prohibition of corporal punishment in the family in its concluding observations on a state party's periodic report, stating:

Given the principle of the dignity of the individual that provides the foundation for international human rights law (see paragraph 41 of the committee 's General Comment No. 13) and in light of Article 10(1) and (3) of the Covenant, the committee recommends that the physical punishment of children in families be prohibited, in line with the recommendation of the Committee on the Rights of the Child.[29]

29. Committee on Economic, Social and Cultural Rights, concluding observations on the UK's Fourth Report under the International Covenant on Economic, Social and Cultural Rights, 17 May 2002, E/C.12/1/Add.79, para. 36: see note 28.

In November 2004, the committee recommended to Malta that it should "consider an explicit prohibition on corporal punishment within the family".[30]

The Committee against Torture

The United Nations Committee against Torture, which is responsible for monitoring implementation of the United Nations Convention against Torture and Other Cruel, Inhuman or Degrading Treatment or Punishment, has also condemned corporal punishment of children.[31]

The Special Rapporteur on Torture of the Commission on Human Rights states in his 2002 report to the UN General Assembly "that any form of corporal punishment of children is contrary to the prohibition of torture and other cruel, inhuman or degrading treatment or punishment". He "therefore calls upon states to take adequate measures, in particular legal and educational ones, to ensure that the right to physical and mental integrity of children is well protected in the public as in the private spheres. He would also welcome information from governmental and non-governmental sources on measures taken to eradicate the practice of corporal punishment against children". The Special Rapporteur draws attention to the condemnation of all corporal punishment by the Committee on the Rights of the Child and by other treaty bodies.[32]

---

30. Committee on Economic, Social and Cultural Rights, concluding observations on Malta's Initial Report under the International Covenant on Economic, Social and Cultural Rights, 26 November 2004, E/C.12/1/Add.101, paras. 22 and 40: see note 28.

31. See, for example, UN General Assembly Official Records, Fiftieth Session, A/50/44, 1995, para. 177 and A/51/44, 1996, para. 65i.

32. Report of the Special Rapporteur against Torture to the UN General Assembly, 2005, A/60/316, 30 August 2005.

2.
Progress towards ending corporal punishment of children in Council of Europe member states

Background to abolition

Centuries ago, the law in many countries defended husbands beating their wives, and masters beating apprentices and servants. The pamphlet that is used to explain the background to the Swedish prohibition of all corporal punishment explains:

> A conception which survived as late as 1920 was that of "domestic disciplining". According to this, the master of every household, following the instructions of the catechism, was to keep the members of his house in good order and chastise those who were disobedient by administering "blows within reason".[33]

The significance of law reform against corporal punishment of children is that it extends the legal protection that adults take for granted to children. The smallest and most fragile of Europe's citizens have had to wait until last for this protection.

English common law (which remains influential in the legislation of at least 70 countries worldwide) includes the defence of "reasonable chastisement". The leading case, still quoted in defence of assaults of children in the UK and many other countries around the world, dates back to 1860. It is left to courts to determine what is "reasonable", and when a parent is prosecuted for assault and uses this defence, it is up to the prosecution to prove that the punishment was not "reasonable".

---

33. Ministry of Justice, Sweden (1979), *Can you bring up children successfully without smacking and spanking?*, pamphlet distributed to all parents and translated into minority languages, including English.

The first country recorded as prohibiting school corporal punishment is Poland, in 1783. By 1900, at least Austria, Belgium and Finland had followed, and the Soviet Union followed suit in 1917. The first recorded attempt to challenge school corporal punishment in the UK had occurred in 1669, when "a lively boy" presented a petition to Parliament "on behalf of the children of this nation", to protest against "that intolerable grievance our youth lie under, in the accustomed severities of the school discipline of this nation".[34] However, it was over two centuries later that the abolition of corporal punishment in the UK began, and it started with the protection of adults.

Flogging in the British army ended in 1906, but remained lawful in the navy until 1957. In 1948, birching was abolished as a judicial punishment. However, it persisted in the Isle of Man, a Crown Dependency of Great Britain, until condemned by the European Court of Human Rights in 1978 (see p. 22); it remained on the statute books in Jersey until 2005 and in Guernsey was still in legislation in 2006, although in practice had ended decades earlier. In 1967 corporal punishment in prisons and borstals (custodial institutions for young offenders) was abolished. Following further decisions of the European Commission and the European Court of Human Rights, corporal punishment in all state-supported education was abolished in 1987; the ban was extended to all schools, by legislation coming into force in 1999 for England and Wales, in 2000 for Scotland and in 2003 for Northern Ireland.

By 2007, corporal punishment had been explicitly prohibited in almost all member states in all schools, including private schools. It has also been prohibited in many countries in the wide range of institutions run by the state and by private or voluntary bodies to provide children with care and treatment outside the family home. In some cases, however, prohibition is through administrative regulation or guidance, rather than primary legislation. In some others, enforcement of prohibition is not rigorous and requires ongoing attention.

---

34. C.B. Freeman (1966), "The children's petition of 1669 and its sequel", *British Journal of Educational Studies*, Vol. 14, p. 216.

In non-institutional forms of care, including foster-care and child-minding, regulation varies and in some countries carers in these settings are assumed to have the same rights as parents to use corporal punishment. (See Appendix 1-online for a summary of the legal status of corporal punishment in each member state.)

Reform to remove parents' rights to use corporal punishment began in the Nordic countries in the 1950s. In Sweden, the criminal law provision excusing parents who caused minor injuries through corporal punishment was removed in 1957 (and at the same time school corporal punishment was abolished – coming into effect in 1958). In 1966 a further legal reform deleted from the Parenthood and Guardianship Code the provision allowing "reprimands"; so from this point on Swedish law did not authorise corporal punishment. In 1969 in Finland the criminal law on assault was amended to remove a provision which stated that a petty assault was not punishable if committed by parents or others exercising their lawful right to chastise a child. In Norway, a similar provision was removed from the Criminal Code in 1972. Austria repealed the explicit authorisation of parental corporal punishment in 1977.

But these states found that repealing a defence to enable the criminal law on assault to apply fully to punitive assaults on children, although a crucial element of law reform to prohibit corporal punishment, was insufficient in itself to send a clear enough signal to society in general to change traditional attitudes and practices. So, as described below, all these and some other member states have gone on to include an explicit prohibition of corporal punishment of children in their civil law.

The 16 member states with explicit abolition of all corporal punishment

By June 2007, 16 member states of the Council of Europe had completed legal reform to prohibit all corporal punishment of children. In these countries, children are protected by the law wherever they are – in their homes, on the streets, in day care, education and all institutions – and whoever the perpetrator. In some of these states, law reform has been accompanied by comprehensive awareness-raising and public education, aimed at achieving full recognition and enjoyment of children's rights to protection. Given population movements, it is clear that this educational process has to be a continuing one.

A number of other states have expressed a commitment to law reform. (see Appendix 1-online).

In a number of other of member states, specific defences still exist to "justify" assaults by parents and some other carers, such as the "reasonable chastisement" defence in English common law and the "right of correction" in legislation elsewhere. In other states, the law does not defend corporal punishment, but lacks explicit prohibition and clear interpretation by politicians and the judiciary that criminal laws on assault apply to punitive assaults on children. Thus, children's rights are not effectively protected. In all states, however, serious assaults are punishable as child abuse.

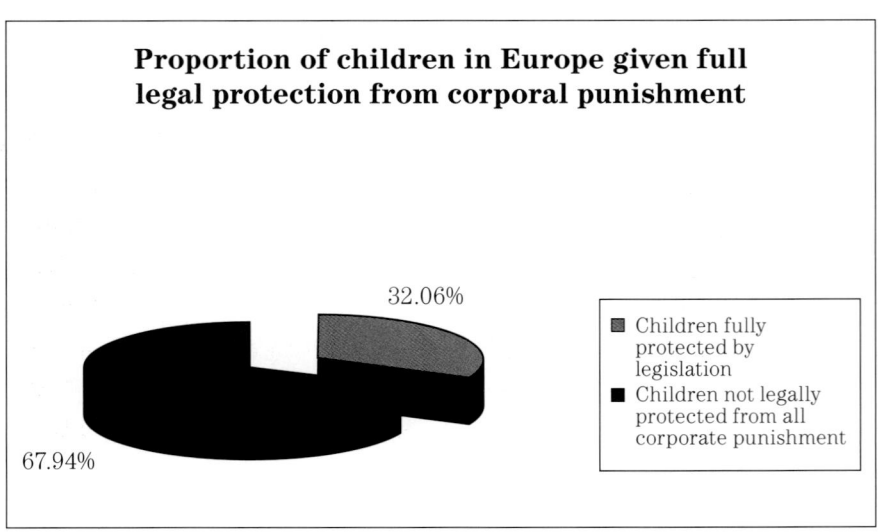

Proportion of children in Europe given full legal protection from corporal punishment

32.06%

67.94%

■ Children fully protected by legislation
■ Children not legally protected from all corporate punishment

Source of population figures (2004): Unicef <http://www.unicef.org> (select "statistics" under "country to country reports") accessed March 2006 (except Cyprus, 2002 Unicef figure)

Sweden

The first country in the world to introduce an explicit prohibition of all corporal punishment and humiliating treatment of children was Sweden. In 1979 a provision was added to the Parenthood and Guardianship Code which now reads: "Children are entitled to care, security and a good upbringing. Children are to be treated with respect for their person and individuality and may not be subjected to corporal punishment or any other humiliating treatment."

Sweden has a history of reforms in this area. In 1957, a provision in the criminal law that excused parents who caused minor injuries through corporal punishment was removed. Abolition of corporal punishment in all schools came into effect in 1958 and in all child care institutions in 1960. In 1966 a provision allowing "reprimands" was deleted from the Parenthood and Guardianship Code. From this point on the law ceased to support parental corporal punishment, but there was no explicit prohibition: opinion polls in the 1970s found there was widespread ignorance of the legal situation, and in 1975 a municipal court acquitted a father of maltreating his three-year-old daughter on the grounds that he had not been proved to have exceeded "the right of corporal chastisement that a guardian has towards a child in his custody".

The Swedish Parliament established in 1977 a Children's Rights Commission, which in its first report, *The child's rights: a prohibition against beating*, unanimously recommended that "an explicit ban on subjecting children to physical punishment or other degrading treatment should be introduced into the Parenthood and Guardianship Code".[35] Following consultation, the government introduced a bill early in 1979 and it was passed by an overwhelming majority of 259 to 6 on 14 March 1979, coming into effect on 1 July.[36] Implementation

---

35. Swedish Children's Rights Commission, first report: *The child's rights: a prohibition against beating*, presented to the Riksdag in autumn 1977.

36. For a longer description of the process of reform in Sweden, see *Ending corporal punishment: Swedish experience of efforts to prevent all forms of violence against children – and the results*, Ministry of Health and Social Affairs and Ministry of Foreign Affairs, Sweden, 2001.

was accompanied by a major and continuing awareness-raising campaign (pp. 95-99). Research has shown a decrease in the extent and severity of corporal punishment experienced by children since prohibition and a marked decline in public support for its use.

Finland

In Finland, the ban on corporal punishment formed part of a comprehensive reform of children's law. The Child Custody and Right of Access Act 1983, which came into force on 1 January 1984, begins with a statement of positive principles of care for children, and continues: "A child shall be brought up in the spirit of understanding, security and love. He shall not be subdued, corporally punished or otherwise humiliated. His growth towards independence, responsibility and adulthood shall be encouraged, supported and assisted."

In 1969, an amendment to the Criminal Code removed a provision on assault which stated that a petty assault was not punishable if committed by parents or others exercising their lawful right to chastise a child. As in Sweden, some confusion remained about the legality of corporal punishment: family law was silent on the issue and a 1978 survey found that 40% of those questioned thought that parents had a legal right to use physical punishment.[37]

When the Child Custody and Right of Access Act was implemented in 1984, it was accompanied by a public education campaign organised by the Ministry of Justice and National Board of Social Affairs and by a major non-governmental organisation, the Central Union for Child Welfare.

Norway

In January 1987, an amendment to the Parent and Child Act took effect. It states: "The child shall not be exposed to physical violence or to treatment which can threaten his physical or mental health."

---

37. P. Vuorista, *The physical punishment of children is inherited*, quoted in T. Peltoniemi, (1983), "Child abuse and physical punishment of children in Finland", *Child Abuse & Neglect*, Vol. 7, p. 33.

In 1972, parents' "right" to use moderate physical punishment had been removed from the assault provisions of the Criminal Code. In 1979 (the International Year of the Child) a governmental committee was established to examine child abuse and neglect; it concluded that the law should be changed to include specific prohibition of all corporal punishment. Norway was the first state to establish through legislation a children's ombudsperson: the Ombudsperson for Children Act was passed in 1981 and the first holder of the post played a major role in lobbying for the specific prohibition of corporal punishment.

Austria

On 15 March 1989 the Austrian Parliament voted to amend its family law and the Youth Welfare Act to state explicitly that in bringing up children "using violence and inflicting physical or mental suffering is unlawful". In 1977 the defence of "reasonable" punishment had been removed from the law on assault. The government has ensured that parents and children have access to advice and counselling, through centres for youth welfare and child protection, as well as telephone help lines for children. Further legislative reforms on violence in the family (1997) enabled injunctions to be taken out to remove men or women committing violence from the family home.

Cyprus

In June 1994 the Cyprus House of Representatives unanimously adopted a new law on the prevention of family violence and protection of victims. This criminalises "the exercise of violence on behalf of any member of the family against another member of the family". The law also includes sanctions relating to the potential psychological damage caused by witnessing violence in the family: it is an offence for violence to occur in the presence of a child. The Advisory Committee for the Prevention and Handling of Violence within the Family has published materials to increase awareness of the legislation and there have been campaigns against family violence by non-governmental organisations and social welfare services. A survey carried out in October 2000 found that 15% of the interviewees still believe that smacking children is an acceptable method of child discipline. The government's response to the questionnaire circulated by the *UN Secretary-General's study on violence against children* (August 2005) stated that the law provided for a "right to administer punishment", but this provision was expected to be removed after review.[38]

Denmark

In May 1997 the Danish Parliament agreed an amendment to the Parental Custody and Care Act, which states: "The child has the right to care and security. He or she shall be treated with respect as an individual and may not be subjected to corporal punishment or any other degrading treatment." In 1985 the Custody and Care Act had been amended to state that "Parental custody implies the obligation to protect the child against physical and psychological violence and against other harmful treatment". This was interpreted by ministers at the time as prohibiting all corporal punishment, but legal textbooks continued to refer to a "right to punish" and judicial interpretations showed continuing confusion. The explicit prohibition was introduced as a result of a campaign by the National Council for Children and Save the Children Denmark. It was accompanied by a major awareness-raising campaign (see pp. 98-99).

Latvia

On 19 June 1998 the Latvian Parliament adopted the Protection of the Rights of the Child Act; this arose from Latvia's ratification of the Convention on the Rights of the Child and from campaigning by non-governmental organisations. The law prohibits cruel treatment, torture and corporal punishment of children, including within the family. Limited awareness-raising and public education, provided by voluntary organisations and media discussion, has accompanied the reform and there has been some increase in the reporting of child abuse.

---

38. Advisory Committee for the Prevention and Handling of Violence within the Family, survey on Cypriots' attitudes to domestic violence and child abuse, October 2000.

Croatia

A new family law came into effect on 1 January 1999. It includes a provision stating that "Parents and other family members must not subject the child to degrading treatment, mental or physical punishment and abuse". The act also requires citizens to inform the authorities of infringements of children's rights. Ratification of the Convention on the Rights of the Child provoked the reform. There was widespread media debate when the law was under discussion, and the media made a major contribution to awareness-raising.

Germany

In July 2000 the Bundestag added a provision to the German Civil Code stating: "Children have the right to a non-violent upbringing. Corporal punishment, psychological injuries and other humiliating measures are prohibited." A new amendment to child-care law imposed a duty on local authorities "to promote ways in which families can resolve conflict without resort to force". As in other countries, this explicit prohibition followed reforms that had removed parents' right to use corporal punishment. A 1998 amendment to the Civil Law had banned "degrading methods of discipline including physical and psychological abuse", but this still fell short of clear prohibition of all corporal punishment, which had been advocated for some time by the KinderKommission (an all-party group of MPs forming a permanent Children's Commission with a full-time staff of civil servants) and by child-protection NGOs. The 2000 reform was accompanied by a public education campaign, led and part-funded by central government, entitled "More respect for children" (for more details, see p. 99).

The first surveys to evaluate the impact of Germany's explicit prohibition of parental corporal punishment in 2000 have found a significant decrease in the prevalence of corporal punishment and a high acceptance of prohibition. In particular, understanding of the legal limits of parental physical sanctions has increased significantly, although there has been insufficient awareness-raising among parents and the general public. Among those parents aware of the new law, there is an increased consciousness of the law's stance on corporal punishment, clearer perception of corporal punishment as violence and more frequent references to the new law in family communication.[39]

Bulgaria

Corporal punishment was prohibited in 2000 by the Child Protection Act which states: "Every child has a right to protection against all methods of upbringing that undermine his or her dignity, against physical, psychical or other types of violence; against all forms of influence, which go against his or her interests." While this is officially seen as abolishing all corporal punishment of children, including in the home, it seems not to have been associated with campaigns to raise public awareness of the prohibition nor with promotion of positive, non-violent alternatives to corporal punishment for parents. Furthermore, the complexity of provisions under the Penal Code for prosecution for violence leading to "trivial" bodily injury limit the legal protection available to children. In 2004, the European Committee of Social Rights deferred its conclusions on Bulgaria's conformity with Article 17 of the Social Charter pending further information on the prohibition of corporal punishment.[40]

Iceland

With the passing of the Children's Act in March 2003, Iceland joined the European countries protecting their children from all corporal punishment in all settings. The Act states: "It is the parents' obligation to protect their child against any physical or mental violence and other degrading or humiliating behaviour." This is interpreted as effectively prohibiting corporal punishment. The Child Protection Act (2002) places obligations on parents "to treat their children with care and consideration", and "to safeguard their welfare at all times".

---

39. K. D. Bussman, "The impact of the German prohibition of violence in education", Halle-Wittenberg: Martin Luther University; surveys funded by the Ministry of Justice and Ministry for Family Affairs, Senior Citizens, Women and Youth.

40. European Committee of Social Rights, 30 September 2004, *Conclusions 2004*, Vol. 1, p. 55.

There is no legal defence available to parents who use corporal punishment, though there is a right to use physical force as an emergency restraint when an individual is in danger of injuring him/herself or others. The Child Protection Act punishes those who "mistreat the child mentally or physically, abuse him/her sexually or otherwise, or neglect the child mentally or physically, so that the child's life or health is at risk", those who inflict "punishments, threats or menaces upon a child that may be expected to harm the child physically or mentally", and "any person who subjects a child to aggressive, abusive or indecent behaviour or hurts or insults him/her".

Ukraine

In Ukraine, a new Family Code came into force in January 2004, prohibiting all corporal punishment. Article 150 of the Code details responsibilities of parents towards their children and states in paragraph 7: "Physical punishment of the child by the parents, as well as other inhuman or degrading treatment or punishment are prohibited".

The Prevention of Domestic Violence Act 2001 also appears to make all violence against children within the family unlawful.

Romania

The Protection and Promotion of the Rights of the Child Act prohibits corporal punishment. The law passed both Chambers of the Romanian Parliament in June 2004 and came into force on 1 January 2005.

In section 1, Civil Rights and Liberties, Article 28 states:

> The child has the right to be shown respect for his or her personality and individuality and may not be made subject to physical punishment or to other humiliating or degrading treatment.

> Disciplinary measures concerning the child can only be taken in accordance with the child's dignity, and, under no circumstances are physical punishments allowed, or punishments which relate to the child's

physical and mental development or which may affect the child's emotional status.

In section 3, Protection of the Child against Abuse and Neglect, Article 90 states:

> It is forbidden to enforce physical punishments of any kind or to deprive the child of his or her rights, which may result in the endangerment of the life, the physical, mental, spiritual, moral and social development, the bodily integrity, and the physical and mental health of the child, both within the family, as well as in any institution which ensures the protection, care and education of children.

Hungary

In December 2004, the Hungarian Parliament enacted an amendment to the Child Protection Act (No. 31/1997), so that a provision in Article 6 now states: "(5) The child has the right to respect for his/her human dignity, to be protected against abuse – physical, sexual and mental violence –, failure to provide care and injury caused by any information. The child shall not be subjected to torture, corporal punishment and any cruel, inhuman or degrading punishment or treatment." The amendment came into force on 1 January 2005.

Greece

In October 2006, the Greek Parliament passed Law 3500/2006 on the Combating of Intra-family Violence, under which corporal punishment of children within the family is prohibited. Article 4 of the new law states: "Physical violence against children as a disciplinary measure in the context of their upbringing brings the consequences of Article 1532 of the Civil Code." Article 1532 of the Civil Code provides for various consequences for abuse of parental authority, the most serious being the removal of parental authority by the courts.

A press release announcing the prohibition, issued by the Greek Ombudsperson (Department of Children's Rights) on 1 November 2006, noted that the Network for the Prevention and Combating of Corporal Punishment of Children – which had been formed specifically to draft the legislation following the collective complaint against Greece under the European Social Charter (see pp. 31-32) – was disappointed that the new law does not specifically use the term "corporal punishment". Nevertheless, that the more general term "physical violence" was intended to include corporal punishment can be seen by the explanatory report accompanying the introduction of the bill to Parliament, which states that "by the provision of Article 4 (of the bill) it is made clear that the corporal punishment of children is not included in the permissible disciplinary measure of Article 1518 of the Civil Code". (Article 1518 of the Civil Code enshrines parents' right to use "corrective measures" but "only if these are necessary from a pedagogic point of view and do not affect the child's dignity".)

The new law came into effect on 24 January 2007.

Netherlands

On 6 March 2007, a new law prohibiting all corporal punishment by parents and carers was passed in the Dutch Senate. The law amends the provisions of the Civil Code on parental authority so that Article 1.247 now states:

> (1) Parental authority includes the duty and the right of the parent to care for and raise his or her minor child. (2) Caring for and raising one's child includes the care and the responsibility for the emotional and physical wellbeing of the child and for his or her safety as well as for the promotion of the development of his or her personality. In the care and upbringing of the child the parents will not use emotional or physical violence or any other humiliating treatment. [Editorial translation]

Article 1.248 of the Code applies Article 1.247 to all other persons acting in loco parentis. The Dutch Cabinet had agreed to proceed with prohibition in February 2005, following a government-commissioned study on the experiences of abolition in other European countries. Department of Justice press releases at the time that "the bill to contribute to the prevention of emotional and physical abuse of children or any other humiliating treatment of children in care and upbringing" was introduced to the Dutch Cabinet stressed that the primary purpose of the new law was "to set a standard". It emphasised that the law would bring the Netherlands into compliance with the UN Convention on the Rights of the Child and Article 17 of the European Social Charter, and address the recommendations made to the Netherlands government by the Committee on the Rights of the Child and the European Committee of Social Rights. A government communication plan to inform parents and the general public about the ban is being prepared. The law came into force in the summer of 2007.

Progress towards abolition in other European states

Italy's Court of Cassation (Supreme Court) in Rome in 1996 declared that parental use of corporal punishment to educate or "correct" children was unlawful. The judgment referred to the Italian Constitution, with its emphasis on respect for the dignity of the individual and repudiation of the use of force to resolve conflicts, and to the Convention on the Rights of the Child. Italy's Penal Code states: "Whoever misuses means of correction or discipline to harm a person subject to his authority, or entrusted to him for purposes of education, instruction, treatment, supervision or custody … shall be punished." The 1996 judgment excludes corporal punishment from acceptable means of correction or discipline. Legislation, however, has not been accordingly reformed. Moreover, there has been no significant awareness-raising concerning the implications of the judgment.

By June 2007, the governments of Lithuania, Luxembourg, Portugal, Slovak Republic, Slovenia and Spain had all stated their intention to pursue law reform to prohibit all corporal punishment.

The European Network of Ombudspersons for Children

The European Network of Ombudspersons for Children (ENOC) was formed in 1997 and by 2007 had grown to include 32 institutions in 23 member states of the Council of Europe. These independent institutions, set up to promote children's rights and interests, aim to work together, sharing strategies and collective approaches, and encouraging the fullest possible implementation of the Convention on the Rights of the Child. In 1999 the network adopted a position statement on ending corporal punishment. This calls on governments and others to work collectively and individually towards ending all corporal punishment of children.

ENOC position statement

The European Network of Ombudspersons for Children urges the governments of all European countries, the European Union, the Council of Europe and other European institutions and non-governmental organisations concerned with children to work collectively and individually towards ending all corporal punishment of children.

As spokespeople for the children of Europe, we believe that eliminating violent and humiliating forms of discipline is a vital strategy for improving children's status as people, and reducing child abuse and all other forms of violence in European societies. This is a long overdue reform, with huge potential for improving the quality of lives and family relationships.

Hitting children is disrespectful and dangerous. Children deserve at least the same protection from violence that we as adults take for granted for ourselves.

While almost all European countries have eliminated corporal punishment from their schools and other institutions for children, it remains common and legally and socially accepted in the family home in most countries. Many states have laws which explicitly defend the rights of parents and other carers to use "reasonable" or "moderate" corporal punishment. Where the law is silent, corporal punishment tends to be accepted in practice.

In a growing minority of countries across Europe, all corporal punishment has been prohibited, often as part of a statement of parents' responsibilities. The purpose of these reforms is not to prosecute more

67

parents, but to send out a clear signal that hitting children is no more acceptable than hitting anyone else.

The United Nations Convention on the Rights of the Child, ratified by all European states, requires legal, educational and other action to protect children from "all forms of physical or mental violence" while in the care of parents and others. The Committee on the Rights of the Child, the international committee of experts responsible for monitoring implementation, has stated that no level of corporal punishment is compatible with the convention and has formally recommended prohibition, coupled with education programmes, to eliminate it.

The Committee of Ministers of the Council of Europe, in a series of recommendations, has condemned corporal punishment and recommended legal reform (see in particular recommendations Nos. R (85) 4; R (90) 2 and R (93) 2).[41]

We urge governments without delay to introduce legislation prohibiting all corporal punishment, and initiate/support education programmes in positive, non-violent forms of discipline. We commit ourselves, as offices committed to improving the lives of all children in Europe, to work actively on this fundamental human rights issue.

---

41. Committee of Ministers adopted texts are found at <http://www.coe.int/t/cm>.

3.
Lifting the veil – making corporal punishment of children visible

Corporal punishment of children in the family remains invisible in many European societies. One indication of the low priority accorded to protecting children from violence in their own homes is the lack of relevant research exposing the extent and serious nature of it. Another is the lack of attention given to children's views and experiences. Chapter 1 documented the human rights obligations that require member states to move immediately to eliminate corporal punishment through explicit law reform. Research may help to build pressure for reform where politicians remain hesitant. Continuing research is required in every state to measure the effectiveness of the measures taken to support law reform with awareness-raising and education, and to review to what extent children's rights are realised.

Parents and children in Europe have been interviewed in depth about their experiences of and attitudes towards violence in the family. Outside the family, few states ensure that children's experiences of violence in all forms of institutional and alternative care are regularly monitored through confidential interviews or questionnaires. Children are seldom asked about their views and experiences of child protection services. The methodologies of the studies that have been undertaken in a minority of countries vary widely, impeding cross-European comparisons.

In countries where corporal punishment by parents remains lawful and socially approved – nearly two thirds of Council of Europe member states in 2007 – interview research finds a majority of children being hit, including babies and very young children. Many are hit frequently – daily or more often – and implements are often used

– belts, sticks, shoes. Most member states still neglect their clear responsibility to ensure effective protection for children.

Statistics of reporting and recording of child abuse and convictions of perpetrators reveal only the tip of the iceberg of violence against children. Children's fundamental human rights are being violated by their care-givers. There is still a long way to go to ensure effective protection for children in a large number of European states.

The figure on p. 56 shows that in 2007 just under one third of Europe's children live in states that have prohibited all corporal punishment. Sweden was the first to initiate legal reforms against parental corporal punishment, in the 1950s, and it appears to be the state that has put most energy into supporting law reform with continuing awareness-raising and public education. Research suggests that these reforms have substantially reduced support for and use of corporal punishment (see pp. 76-78). The following section summarises the results of some of the larger prevalence studies in member states.[42]

Accumulating evidence of corporal punishment's ill-effects

While the imperative for law reform to prohibit all corporal punishment in member states is first and foremost one of human rights, there is substantial and growing research literature demonstrating that corporal punishment is consistently associated with numerous negative outcomes for children. A landmark meta-analysis of 88 studies of the correlates of typical forms of corporal punishment by Elizabeth Thompson Gershoff, published in 2002, demonstrates that corporal punishment predicts numerous negative outcomes and no positive long-term outcomes.[43] It is a predictor of poorer child mental health (12 of 12 studies), eroded parent-child relationships (13 of 13 studies), weaker internalisation of moral standards (13 of 15 studies), increased child aggression (27 of 27 studies), and

---

42. For summaries of other published research see the website of the Global Initiative to End All Corporal Punishment of Children: <http://www.endcorporalpunishment.org>.

43. E.T. Gershoff (2002), "Corporal punishment by parents and associated child behaviours and experiences: A meta-analytic and theoretical review", *Psychological Bulletin*, Vol. 128 (4), pp. 539-579.

increased child anti-social behaviour (11 of 12 studies). Furthermore, these outcomes persist into adulthood. Corporal punishment is associated with poorer adult mental health (8 of 8 studies) and higher levels of adult criminal and antisocial behaviour (4 of 5 studies).

An important finding of the research literature is that corporal punishment is closely tied to family violence in several ways. First, most physical abuse is corporal punishment.[44] Corporal punishment was found to be a risk factor for physical harm in all of the 10 studies of this relationship examined in the 2002 meta-analysis by Gershoff. The intensity of corporal punishment can easily escalate, both within a single incident and over time. In fact, children who are physically punished are many times more likely to experience severe violence than those who are not punished physically.[45] Second, the experience of corporal punishment early in life can alter one's definition of "violence". Individuals who have been severely punished may grow up to believe that their experiences were normal.[46] These perceptions, in turn, increase the likelihood of maltreatment continuing. Indeed, Gershoff's meta-analysis reveals that children who are physically punished are more likely to grow up to abuse their own children or spouses (5 of 5 studies).

Research on corporal punishment's prevalence in the family

Croatia

Over 1 000 undergraduate students at the University of Zagreb, aged 18 to 29, were surveyed during 1997 and 1998 (before prohibition of corporal punishment took effect on 1 January 1999) on their childhood experiences of physical and sexual abuse and also of witnessing

---

44. D.G. Gil (1970), *Violence against children: physical child abuse in the United States* (Cambridge, MA: Harvard University Press); A. Kadushin and J.A. Martin (1981), *Child abuse: an interactional event* (New York: Columbia University Press); N. Trocmé et al. (2001), *Canadian incidence study of reported child abuse and neglect* (Ottawa: National Clearinghouse on Family Violence).

45. M.E. Clément et al. (2000), *La violence familiale dans la vie des enfants du Québec* (Québec: Institut de la Statistique du Québec).

46. J.F. Knutson and M.B. Selner (1994), "Punitive childhood experiences reported by young adults over a 10-year period", *Child Abuse & Neglect*, Vol. 18 (2), pp. 155-166.

violence between adults in their homes. Overall, 93% reported corporal punishment or abuse; 27% reported assaults causing injury; 40% had witnessed violence between adults in the family. Just over a third reported that they had never been hit with an implement, while 40% had been hit "rarely" and 20% "sometimes; several times a year". Only 18% said they had never been slapped on the face; 45% had been slapped "rarely" and 30% "sometimes; several times a year".[47]

Georgia

A study in 2000 by the Red Cross Committee of Georgia of physical and psychological violence against children in the family, institutions (schools, study groups, sport groups) and neighbourhoods used structured interviews with 4 382 children aged 6-17. Almost two in five (39.2%) reported being subjected to corporal punishment in the family, mostly by the mother.[48]

Germany

Government research was undertaken in 2001 and published in 2003 into the reception and initial impact of the prohibition of corporal punishment in child-rearing in November 2000. Interviews were held nationwide with 3 000 parents of children below 18 years and 2 000 young people aged 12-18. Surveys were also administered to 1 074 government and non-governmental institutions, with 30 representatives of relevant institutions interviewed in depth. The research found that around 28% of parents rarely resorted to disciplinary sanctions and "as far as possible" did not use corporal punishment; 54% frequently used "minor" but never "serious" corporal punishment (such as beatings and spankings); 17% frequently used "serious" corporal punishment, including beatings and spankings, as well

47. N. Pecnik (2003), *Intergenerational transmission of child abuse* (in Croatian), Slap: Jastrebarsko.

48. Red Cross Committee of Georgia (2000), "Child abuse and neglect", Red Cross/Unicef.

as psychological punishments. Boys were more commonly hit than girls, and more commonly experienced "serious" corporal punishment. Based on parents' reports, in comparison with previous studies the report notes a substantial decrease in corporal punishment at all degrees of severity. For example, in 1996 a third of parents (33.2%) reported they had hit their child's bottom, compared with just over a quarter (26.4%) in 2001.[49]

Greece

A 1993 study in Greece found that in a national cohort of 8 158 children aged 7, one in three (37.7%) was spanked at least once a week and one in six daily (18%).[50]

Research carried out between 1994 and 1997 at the Department of Family Relations in the Institute of Child Health in Athens, involving 591 structured interviews with mothers of 6-year-old and 12-year-old schoolchildren, revealed that 65.5% of mothers used physical punishment to discipline their children, with mothers of 6-year-olds three times more likely to use such punishment than mothers of 12-year-olds.[51] Of the mothers interviewed, 62% believed that physical punishment is used by most parents, and 82% believed that at least half of all parents hit their children. Of those children physically punished, 4% suffered minor injuries and 1.2% suffered injuries needing stitches and/or hospitalisation.[52]

---

49. Federal Ministry of Justice and Federal Ministry for Family Affairs, Senior Citizens, Women and Youth (2003), *Violence in upbringing: an assessment after the introduction of the right to a non-violent upbringing.*

50. H. Agathonos-Georgopoulou (1997), "Child maltreatment in Greece: a review of research", *Child Abuse Review*, Vol. 6, pp. 257-271.

51. I. Fereti and M. Stavrianki (1997), "The use of physical punishment in the Greek family: selected socio-demographic aspects", *International Journal of Child and Family Welfare*, Vol. 3, pp. 206-216.

52. I. Fereti (2002), "Initiatives to reduce and prevent corporal punishment of children within the family in Greece", Athens: Institute of Child Health.

Poland

Corporal punishment of children is generally socially accepted.[53] Child maltreatment is most common in children below the age of 3, and affects more girls than boys.[54]

A nationwide survey of adults in 2001 found that 80% had experienced beatings in the home as children, by parents or guardians, more commonly for men than for women.[55] The study found that the higher the level of education of respondents, the less often they had experienced physical punishment and the less frequently they used corporal punishment on their own children. Corporal punishment was most often used on children aged 7-14. The majority of people who experienced corporal punishment in their childhood felt it had been effective, but 48% of respondents believed that corporal punishment by parents should be banned. The survey found that 20% of adult respondents had also experienced corporal punishment by teachers during their childhood.

Romania

A number of studies of the prevalence of physical abuse of children were carried out in 2000. Research by Save the Children Romania found that, of a sample of 423 children aged 11-13, 75% had been subjected to corporal punishment, with 5% reporting that they needed medical treatment following the abuse.[56] A national survey of 1 556 households with children, 1 295 schoolchildren aged 13-14, and 110 professionals from different fields, found that 47% of parents admitted to using corporal punishment as a disciplinary method while 84% of children stated that they had been subjected to corporal punishment by their parents, including 20% who reported being

53. G. Fluderska and M. Sajkowska (2001), *The problem of child abuse in Poland: attitudes and experiences*, Warsaw: Nobody's Children Foundation; Helsinki Foundation for Human Rights (1994), *Children's rights in Poland*, Helsinki: HFHR.

54. B. Mossakowska (1996), "Medical observation on child abuse", *Child abuse & neglect*, Vol. 20 (2).

55. G. Fluderska and M. Sajkowska (2001), *The problem of child abuse in Poland: attitudes and experiences*, Warsaw: Nobody's Children Foundation.

56. G. Alexandrescu et al. (2000), *Child abuse and neglect*, Save the Children Romania.

beaten with objects and 15% who were afraid to go home because of the beatings.[57]

In addition, an opinion poll of 1 200 children aged 8-13, carried out by Save the Children Romania during the national campaign "Beating is not from Heaven" in 2002, found that 81% thought beating was an inefficient method of education, 70% believed that child protection against violence was inadequate, 76% believed that adults should be punished by the state for beating children and 83% felt that corporal punishment should be prohibited by law.

Slovak Republic

Research by the Bratislava International Centre for Family Studies in 2000, involving 2 433 children aged 13-17, found the following prevalence of corporal punishment in the family: beating by parents was said to occur "very often" for 0.3% of children, "often" for 0.9%, "rarely" for 14.1%, and "never" for 73%. Parental slaps were said to occur "very often" for 0.5%, "often" for 1.9%, "rarely" for 35%, and "never" for 52.9%.[58]

Attitudinal research by the Bratislava International Centre for Family Studies, undertaken in 2002, sampled 856 adults.[59] Preliminary analysis revealed that 98.6% believed that parents should be allowed to use a "smack on the buttock from time to time"; 75.3% believe that parents should be allowed to use "occasional slaps"; 41.7% believed that occasional beating with an implement was acceptable; 22.9% believed that repeated beating is acceptable.

United Kingdom

The Department of Health in the United Kingdom commissioned a large-scale "community study of physical violence to children in

---

57. K. Browne et al. (2002), *Child abuse and neglect in Romanian families: A National Prevalence Study, 2000*, Romanian National Authority for Child Protection.

58. International Centre for Family Studies (2002), "The children's rights applying in the praxis. Preliminary survey report", Bratislava: International Centre for Family Studies.

59. International Centre for Family Studies (2003, in progress), "The prevalence of violence in Slovakia", Bratislava: International Centre for Family Studies.

the home and associated variables" in the 1990s.[60] Carried out by Marjorie Smith, Gavin Nobes and others, it found a very high frequency of physical punishments, including severe punishment. The large majority (91%) of children had been hit. Frequency of hitting declined with age. Only 25% of the babies aged up to 1-year in the study had never been smacked by their mothers, and 14% of 1-year-olds had been smacked with "moderate" severity; 38% had been smacked more than once a week. The study included interviews with both parents in 99 two-parent families. It was found that one fifth of children in these families had been hit with an implement and over one third of children (35%) had at some time experienced a punishment that was rated as "severe" (defined as punishments "that were intended to, had the potential to, or actually did cause physical and/ or psychological injury or harm to the child").

While one quarter of individual parents reported physically punishing their child at least weekly, nearly half the children (46%) reported being physically punished this frequently. A total of 52% of 1-year-old children, 48% of 4-year-olds, 35% of 7-year-olds and 11% of 11-year-olds were hit/smacked weekly or more often by their parents. Three children, all 1-year-old, were reportedly hit/smacked daily or more often by a parent.

Research on the impact of Sweden's law reforms

The Swedish Government has backed successive law reforms with public education and awareness-raising and has also commissioned opinion and other research over the last few decades to measure the effects of the reforms. A review of available research by Canadian Professor Joan E. Durrant in 2000 concluded that public support for corporal punishment had declined markedly: "This decline is most dramatic among the younger generation of today's parents; only

---

60. G. Nobes et al. (1997), "Physical punishment of children in two-parent families", *Clinical child psychology and psychiatry,* Vol. 2 (2), pp. 271-281.

six per cent of Swedes under the age of 35 currently support the use of corporal punishment."[61]

Professor Durrant noted that, in contrast to trends in many other countries, in Sweden the proportion of young people who consume alcohol has been decreasing steadily since 1971, as has the proportion of youth who have experimented with drugs. The proportion of young people who continue to use drugs is negligible. The rate of youth suicide also declined between 1970 and 1996: "While drawing a direct causal link between the corporal punishment ban and any of these social trends would be too simplistic, the evidence presented here indicates that the ban has not had negative effects. In terms of its original goals of modifying public attitudes toward corporal punishment and facilitating early identification and supportive intervention, it has certainly been successful." Reporting of assaults on children has increased, as it has over this period in every country, but there has been a declining trend in prosecution and compulsory interventions in the family.

The most recent studies in Sweden were commissioned in 2000 by a Committee on Child Abuse and Related Issues, established by the Swedish Parliament. They comprised interviews with parents of 1 609 children about their use of corporal punishment in bringing up their children, a nationwide classroom questionnaire completed by 1 764 children aged 11-13 about their experiences of and attitudes to corporal punishment and bullying, and a nationwide postal survey completed by 1 576 20-year-olds about their experiences of and attitudes to corporal punishment, bullying and sexual abuse.

A report on these and earlier studies shows that it is not only the absolute number of children subjected to corporal punishment that has decreased; children who are subjected to it experience it much less often than before.[62] The study found that "violent corporal

61. J.E. Durrant (2000), *A generation without smacking: the impact of Sweden's ban on physical punishment*, Save the Children UK.

62. J. Staffan (2002), *Children and abuse – corporal punishment and other forms of child abuse in Sweden at the end of the second millennium: A scientific report prepared for the Committee on Child Abuse and Related Issues*, Ministry of Health and Social Affairs, Sweden.

punishment of children which could potentially cause serious injury has also decreased substantially". Four per cent of children aged 11-13 and 7% of young adults (aged 20) state they have been subjected to more severe corporal punishment with some sort of implement on at least one occasion in their lives. The report notes that schoolchildren's attitudes to corporal punishment have become significantly more negative: "The proportion of pupils who can accept being hit by a parent decreased from 50% to 20% between 1995 and 2000. The cause of this dramatic change in attitude during the latter part of the 1990s cannot be established with full certainty. It is clear, however, that schoolchildren are much more aware of their civil rights now than they used to be, partly due to information on the UN Convention on the Rights of the Child as provided in schools and by non-governmental organisations."

Researching children's views and experiences

The people most affected by corporal punishment are children, yet they are rarely involved in relevant debates. However, in November 2002, the Council of Europe's Forum on Children and Families involved young people in a seminar on "Corporal punishment in the family",[63] as part of the Council's project "Responses to violence in everyday life in a democratic society". The young people came from Azerbaijan, Cyprus, Czech Republic, Denmark and United Kingdom. James Anderson, Adult Support Worker for Article 12, a self-advocacy organisation of children and young people, and Laura Dent from Right Here, Right Now, another body led by young people, presented research studies of children's views on corporal punishment in the UK.[64] They underlined that it is fundamental that the views and experiences of younger children should be heard because they are often forgotten or ignored. They told the seminar that children very clearly see this issue in a different way from adults; for example,

---

63. For a full report of the seminar, see Council of Europe document CS-Forum (2002) 13 Addendum.

64. For details of these organisations, see <http://www.article12.com/ and http://www.rhrn.org.uk>/.

"most adults say that smacking doesn't really hurt, but children have said things like 'It feels as if someone banged you with a hammer'". Adults also use special words like "smacking" for corporal punishment, but in fact most children see a smack as a hit.

Under the UN Convention on the Rights of the Child, states must assure children the right to express their views freely "in all matters affecting the child", the views of the child being given "due weight" in accordance with age and maturity (Article 12). Thus it is an obligation to facilitate the involvement in the process of eliminating corporal punishment. When the Committee on the Rights of the Child held a discussion day on violence against children in the family and schools, in September 2001, one of its proposals was that: "In conceptualising violence, the committee recommends that the critical starting point and frame of reference be the experience of children themselves. Therefore children and young people must be meaningfully involved in promoting and strategising action on violence against children."[65] In September 2006, the Committee on the Rights of the Child held a discussion day on the right of the child to be heard, which aimed at exploring the meaning of Article 12 of the convention and its implications for children as individuals and as a group.[66]

Unicef survey on children's experience of violence

A wide-ranging Unicef opinion survey, conducted in 2001, displayed a preliminary impression of children's experiences.[67] It included 15 200 interviews representative of the 93 million 9-17-year-olds in 35 countries in Europe and Central Asia. Data were disaggregated according to factors such as region, gender and age.

---

65. Committee on the Rights of the Child, General Discussion Day on Violence against Children in the Family and in Schools, September 2001, Report on the 28th Session, September/October 2001, CRC/C/111; see <http://www.unhchr.ch>.

66. The recommendations adopted following the discussion are available at <http://www. ohchr.org/english/bodies/crc/docs/discussion/Final _ Recommendations _ after _ DGD. doc>.

67. Unicef (2001), *Young voices opinion survey of children and young people in Europe and Central Asia.*

The results revealed that 59% of children experience violent or aggressive behaviour within their families. Reports of such behaviour tended to be higher in eastern and central Europe, as well as Central Asia: 61% of children in these regions reported violence. The corresponding percentage for western Europe was 54%.

Children further reported that parents scold, insult or beat them when they do something "wrong". More than one in ten (11%) of the children stated that it happens "very/quite often".

Nevertheless, it appears that children's belief in the value of non-violent means of conflict resolution remains widespread and strong. In responding to the question, "Is talking a good solution to problems?", the overwhelming majority of children answered in the affirmative: 47% asserted that talking is "always" a good solution and a further 35% stated that it is "often" a good solution. Interestingly, statistics revealed similar views among children of varying age groups. However, a difference on the basis of gender was evident: whereas 51% of girls in all countries affirmed that talking is "always" a good solution to problems, only 44% of boys shared this belief.

Similarly, children's responses to the question, "Is shouting a good solution to problems?" demonstrated a preference for non-violent mediation: 58% of children responded that shouting is "never" a solution and another 24% considered it to be only "rarely" a solution. Feedback on the following question, "Is hitting a good solution to problems?", further emphasises children's aversion to violence: 79% of all children affirmed that such actions are "never" a solution and 11% stated that hitting is "rarely" a solution. Again, there was a clear gender-related difference in the results: 83% of girls stated that hitting was "never" a good solution, but only 75% of boys held this view.

Children were subsequently questioned on their participation in family decision-making, which can be a revealing factor in dynamics relating to the presence of violence in the family. Upon being asked "Is my opinion considered when decisions concerning me are made at home?", 57% of all children replied in the affirmative. It is significant that statistics on this question were identical throughout all the regions surveyed.

Young children's views in England

At the end of 1998 the Department of Health in England announced that it intended to consult the public on physical punishment in the family. This followed a judgment of the European Court of Human Rights that UK law failed to protect a young boy whose stepfather beat him with a garden cane; see pp. 23-24) but it made no attempt to consult children. So two non-governmental organisations, the National Children's Bureau and Save the Children, decided to carry out a unique consultation on smacking with 5- to 7-year-old children.[68]

The two project workers, who were both experienced in consulting children, decided from the outset that children would not be informed about the organisations' position on smacking. Children were told they were the experts on smacking; the project workers also stressed the importance of children sharing their own individual thoughts and responses rather than copying their friends' answers. During 1998, 16 small group discussions were held with 76 children aged 5 to 7 (there was one 4-year-old) in six schools and two summer play schemes. In 14 of the 16 discussions, a teacher or other school/play scheme representative was present throughout. Parents were fully briefed in advance and gave written permission for children to take part. Children's consent was obtained at the beginning of the discussions, when they were advised that they could opt out at any stage of the proceedings (either by leaving the room or not answering particular questions). Only four children – all 5-year-olds – decided not to complete the group discussion.

A community artist was commissioned to create a storybook whose central character, Splodge, was an alien, introduced to children as not knowing much about our world. To help Splodge understand

---

68. C. Willow and T. Hyder (1998), *It hurts you inside – children talking about smacking*, National Children's Bureau and Save the Children.

smacking, a series of questions was put to groups of children, which individual children answered in turn. Splodge's questions were:

- Who knows what a smack is?

- Why do you think children get smacked?

- Who usually smacks children?

- Where do children usually get smacked?

- What does it feel like to be smacked?

- How do children act after being smacked? How do adults act after they have given a smack?

- Adults smack children, but why don't children smack adults? Children smack each other, but why don't adults smack each other?

- When you are big, do you think you will smack children?

- Do you know anybody who doesn't like smacking? Who thinks it is wrong to smack?

- How can we stop children being smacked?

The consultation produced nine major messages from the children:

- Children defined smacking as hitting; most of them described a smack as a hard or very hard hit.

- Children said smacking hurts.

- Children are the main people who dislike smacking, followed by parents, friends and grandparents; the vast majority of the children who took part thought smacking was wrong.

- Children respond negatively to being smacked, and adults regret smacking.

- The children said parents and other grown-ups are the people who mostly smack children.

- Children said they usually get smacked indoors and on the bottom, arm or head.

- Children are smacked because: they have been violent themselves; they have been naughty or mischievous; they have broken or spoiled things; or because they have disobeyed or failed to listen to their parents.

- Children said that children do not smack adults because they are scared they will be hit again; some adults who riot smack each other, whereas others, who are big, know better and love and care about each other and do not smack each other.

- Half the children involved in the consultation said they will not smack children when they are adults; 5-year-olds most often said they will not smack children when they are big.

Children's views in Scotland

Between March and November 2000, Save the Children researched the opinions of 1 319 children and young people in Scotland aged 6-18 (most aged 8-12), using focus groups and questionnaires.[69] Of the 1 249 children aged 8-18 who completed the questionnaire, 93% said there were other ways that parents could discipline children without resorting to violence; 76% believed it was wrong for a parent or other adult to hit a child. They believed that hitting was the result of a parent's feelings of anger, stress and frustration, rather than a reasonable act; they used over 40 adjectives to describe how distressed they felt when they had been hit by a parent or other adult. They felt it was a bad example, and contradicted teaching them that hitting other people was wrong. Children were aware of the physical difference in strength between adults and children and that hitting could lead to physical injury.

---

69. E. Cutting (2001), *"It doesn't sort anything": A report on the views of children and young people about the use of physical punishment*, Edinburgh: Save the Children.

Children's views in Northern Ireland

Save the Children in Northern Ireland asked 189 children aged 4-11 in after-school clubs what they thought about smacking.[70] Face-to-face interviews were carried out with 68 children, and 121 children provided written answers to four questions:

• Why do you think adults hit children?

• How do you think a child feels after being hit by a parent or other adult?

• When children do something wrong, do you think there are other ways of sorting things out instead of hitting them? If yes, what do you suggest?

• Do you think that it is wrong for an adult to hit a child?

Two-thirds of the children believed that children were hit because they are "bad, bold, cheeky, doing things wrong or doing wrong things", with nearly all children aged 8 or under thinking children get hit because they are bad. One in four children believed that children get hit because of how the adult is feeling rather than because of what the child does. Very few thought they were hit in order to teach them anything.

When asked how they feel when they are hit, more than 80% of children used words like "hurt", "sad", "sore", "upset", "unhappy", "unloved", "heartbroken", "awful" and "nobody loves them". Only two children, boys aged 9 and 10, said they did not mind being hit. Most children (94%) said they would not smack their children when they themselves became parents. Most children thought it was wrong for an adult to hit a child, mainly because it hurts the child and it sets a bad example. Fewer than 3 in 20 thought it was acceptable.

---

70. G. Horgan (2002), "It's a hit, not a 'smack': A booklet about what children think about being hit or smacked by adults", Belfast: Save the Children.

Children's views in Wales

Research by Save the Children into the views of 77 children aged 4-10 in Wales produced findings similar to those in the research in England, Scotland and Northern Ireland.[71]

---

71. A. Crowley, and C. Vulliamy (2002), *Listen up! Children talk: About smacking*, Cardiff: Save the Children.

4.
Eliminating corporal punishment of children – the process

The human rights obligations of member states require that their domestic law prohibits all corporal punishment and other degrading or humiliating treatment or punishment of children. In addition, they are responsible for implementing effective measures to ensure the realisation of children's right to protection. There is ample experience across member states of successive legal reforms – accompanied by measures to educate the general public and raise awareness – to demonstrate how to make progress towards effective protection. It is clear that the process must be ongoing, not one-off, and there must be regular and sensitive monitoring of children's experiences of violence, in their homes and other settings, and of child protection services.

Law reform to abolish all corporal punishment

Every member state of the Council of Europe should ensure the safeguarding of all children's rights to respect for their human dignity and physical integrity and to equal protection under the law. Every country has laws that criminalise assaults. Respecting children's rights requires that the law on assault applies equally to punitive assaults on children. Any defences or justifications that may exist in criminal and civil law must be removed. In common-law countries, any common-law defence (defences developed by court decisions, like the "reasonable punishment" defence in English law) should also be explicitly removed.

In addition, as the European Committee of Social Rights has made clear in its general observation on corporal punishment and Article 17 of the European Social Charter (see Chapter 1, p. 28), "any other form of degrading punishment or treatment of children must be prohibited in legislation and combined with adequate sanctions in penal or civil law". There are other ways of punishing children that do not involve the use of physical force, but which can be very damaging: humiliating children, constant blaming or sarcasm or ridicule, isolating children, withdrawing food or other necessities and so on.

Experience in several member states has indicated that simply removing any existing defences in law does not send a strong enough message to parents and others that corporal punishment is prohibited. In any case, in some European countries, although there is no explicit legal defence available to parents or other carers, corporal punishment remains common and socially approved. This is why (as described in Chapter 2) 16 member states have implemented explicit prohibition of corporal punishment in family law or parenting codes. As the purpose of such laws is to change attitudes and practice within the private arena of the family, they send the clearest possible signal. Having an explicit and well-publicised legal framework acts as a deterrent and as the essential basis for public education. It enables those working with families in health, education and social services, including child protection services, to deliver an unequivocal message that hitting and humiliating children is unlawful.

Box 4 – Law reform: the essential steps

• Ensuring there are no existing defences, in statute or common law, that justify corporal punishment by parents or others;

• Ensuring that the criminal law on assault applies equally to punitive assaults on children;

• Enacting explicit prohibition of all corporal punishment and all other degrading or humiliating treatment or punishment of children, normally in civil law;

• Providing guidance on appropriate enforcement of these laws, which focuses on protection and promotion of the human rights of children in general and on the best interests of affected children in particular;

• Ensuring comprehensive awareness-raising of the existence of these laws among children, all who live and work with them and among the general public.

Children, and particularly young children, are not in a good position to challenge assaults by their parents and other carers. So traditional patterns of child-rearing, involving violent punishment and humiliation, continue to be passed on from generation to generation. Without extensive awareness-raising and public education, these culturally-embedded methods of raising children cannot be changed.

Enforcing abolition

All member states have laws criminalising serious assaults on children. All have child protection systems that enable children to be separated from their parents when this is the only way to protect them from physical, emotional or sexual violence or neglect. Ensuring that the law criminalises all corporal punishment of children and making the public aware of children's rights to protection will be likely to lead to increased reporting of violence against children. The public, and those working with families, will become more sensitised to violence against children and to children's right to protection. Increased awareness and reporting do not have to mean increases in prosecutions or formal, compulsory interventions in the family. Given children's special and dependent status, the prosecution of their parents and separation from them is unlikely to be in children's best interests, except in very exceptional cases.

The repeal of any defences that parents or other carers could use to justify assaulting children will make prosecution and formal child protection interventions easier in those cases where these appear to be the only way to protect children. "Trivial" assaults on adults are not in general prosecuted and the same will be true of such assaults on children. There are also obvious evidential difficulties in bringing prosecutions for assaults on babies and young children, who appear to receive the most corporal punishment.

In countries where corporal punishment has been explicitly prohibited, there are no reports of problems over prosecution policy or practice. In Sweden, where abolition has been in force for the longest time, reporting of child abuse has increased substantially with a general, growing sensitivity to the problem of violence against children. At the same time, there has been a declining trend in the proportion of reports leading to prosecution.

Some opponents suggest that a law to ban corporal punishment will turn children against their parents, cause thousands of additional prosecutions and unnecessary separation of children from parents. However, prosecution policy, focused carefully on the best interests of the child and on the public interest, can prevent any unintended effects. Critics also question the point of a law that is "unenforceable". In fact, this law is as enforceable as other laws challenging violence between adults within the family. Its primary purpose is preventive – to stop parents and others from assaulting children – rather than to respond punitively after the event; to move people on from believing that hitting children is just or safe to more positive and respectful relationships with children.

Implementing laws against corporal punishment within the family

In its General Comment No. 8 (2006),[72] the Committee on the Rights of the Child gives detailed advice on implementation of prohibition of corporal punishment in the family (paras. 38-43):

> The committee believes that implementation of the prohibition of all corporal punishment requires awareness-raising, guidance and training ... for all those involved. This must ensure that the law operates in the best interests of the affected children – in particular when parents or other close family members are the perpetrators. The first purpose of law reform to prohibit corporal punishment of children within the family is prevention: to prevent violence against children by changing attitudes and practice, underlining children's right to equal protection and providing an unambiguous foundation for child protection and for the promotion of positive, non-violent and participatory forms of child-rearing.

---

72. General Comment No. 8 is found at <http://www.ohchr.org/english/bodies/crc/comments. htm>.

Achieving a clear and unconditional prohibition of all corporal punishment will require varying legal reforms in different states parties. It may require specific provisions in sectoral laws covering education, juvenile justice and all forms of alternative care. But it should be made explicitly clear that the criminal law provisions on assault also cover all corporal punishment, including in the family. This may require an additional provision in the criminal code of the state party. But it is also possible to include a provision in the civil code or family law, prohibiting the use of all forms of violence, including all corporal punishment. Such a provision emphasizes that parents or other caretakers can no longer use any traditional defence that it is their right ("reasonably" or "moderately") to use corporal punishment if they face prosecution under the criminal code. Family law should also positively emphasise that parental responsibility includes providing appropriate direction and guidance to children without any form of violence.

The principle of equal protection of children and adults from assault, including within the family, does not mean that all cases of corporal punishment of children by their parents that come to light should lead to prosecution of parents. The de minimis principle – that the law does not concern itself with trivial matters – ensures that minor assaults between adults only come to court in very exceptional circumstances; the same will be true of minor assaults on children. States need to develop effective reporting and referral mechanisms. While all reports of violence against children should be appropriately investigated and their protection from significant harm assured, the aim should be to stop parents from using violent or other cruel or degrading punishments through supportive and educational, not punitive, interventions.

Children's dependent status and the unique intimacy of family relations demand that decisions to prosecute parents, or to formally intervene in the family in other ways, should be taken with very great care. Prosecuting parents is in most cases unlikely to be in their children's best interests. It is the committee's view that prosecution and other formal interventions (for example, to remove the child or remove the perpetrator) should only proceed when they are regarded both as necessary to protect the child from significant harm and as being in the best interests of the affected child. The affected child's views should be given due weight, according to his or her age and maturity.

Advice and training for all those involved in child protection systems, including the police, prosecuting authorities and the courts, should underline this approach to enforcement of the law. Guidance should also emphasize that article 9 of the convention requires that any separation of the child from his or her parents must be deemed necessary in the best interests of the child and be subject to judicial review, in accordance with applicable law and procedures, with all interested parties, including the child, represented. Where separation is deemed to be justified, alternatives to placement of the child outside the family should be considered, including removal of the perpetrator, suspended sentencing, and so on.

Where, despite prohibition and positive education and training programmes, cases of corporal punishment come to light outside the family home – in schools, other institutions and forms of alternative care, for example – prosecution may be a reasonable response. The threat to the perpetrator of other disciplinary action or dismissal should also act as a clear deterrent. It is essential that the prohibition of all corporal punishment and other cruel or degrading punishment, and the sanctions that may be imposed if it is inflicted, should be well disseminated to children and to all those working with or for children in all settings. Monitoring disciplinary systems and the treatment of children must be part of the sustained supervision of all institutions and placements which is required by the convention. Children and their representatives in all such placements must have immediate and confidential access to child-sensitive advice, advocacy and complaints procedures and ultimately to the courts, with necessary legal and other assistance. In institutions, there should be a requirement to report and to review any violent incidents.

Another objection sometimes raised against law reform to prohibit corporal punishment is that it will prevent parents using physical actions to protect and to restrain their children. Parents should certainly be reassured that law reforms to prohibit corporal punishment and deliberate humiliation do not interfere in any way with positive or protective physical actions. When Sweden implemented an explicit ban on all corporal punishment in 1979, the explanatory booklet sent to all parents stated: "The law therefore now forbids all forms of physical punishment of children, including smacking and the like, although it goes without saying that you can still snatch a child away from a hot stove or open window if there is a risk of its injuring itself."[73]

Awareness-raising and public education

While law reform is fundamental to recognising children's human rights, it will not on its own achieve effective protection of all children. Law reform needs to be well-publicised and clearly and positively interpreted by politicians, community leaders and the judiciary as prohibiting all corporal punishment and deliberate humiliation of children. It needs to be accompanied by continuing efforts to raise awareness of children's rights to protection and continuing education of public and parents to promote positive forms of child-rearing and education.

Attempts to "educate" society away from using corporal punishment while the law continues to condone it are unlikely to have much success. Politicians, responding to human rights obligations, need to lead public opinion; in doing so they can be confident from the experience of states that have abolished all corporal punishment that public opinion quickly shifts to support the reforms.

Ways of promoting the prohibition of all corporal punishment

In 1981, just two years after Sweden's explicit ban on all corporal punishment came into effect, research found that 96% of the population knew that corporal punishment was forbidden; only 1% believed it was still permitted. In fact corporal punishment had been criminalised since the 1950s, but in 1971 polls found that less than two thirds

---

73. Ministry of Justice, Sweden (1979), *Can you bring up children successfully without smacking and spanking?*, pamphlet distributed to all parents and translated into minority languages, including English.

of the population knew it was illegal.[74] So Sweden's awareness-raising campaign was certainly successful, though the most recent research underlines the need for educational activities to continue.[75]

The United Nations Convention on the Rights of the Child requires states that have ratified it (all member states of the Council of Europe) to "make the principles and provisions of the convention widely known, by appropriate and active means, to adults and children alike" (Article 42). Awareness-raising about law reform and children's rights can be built into the school curriculum, at all levels and in creative ways, and into initial and in-service training of all those who work with and for families and children. Professionals, who have all been children and many of whom are parents, may hold traditional attitudes that condone corporal punishment and will need to understand the law and their obligations to promote positive, non-violent forms of discipline.

In all states there are health programmes targeted at new parents and these can include promotion of children's rights and the law, as well as knowledge of child development and the dangers of corporal punishment; health visitors, doctors and paediatricians can play a crucial role in dissemination. Understanding child development and promoting positive discipline is a key part of parenting education. Day-care workers can both practise and promote positive discipline.

Moves to end corporal punishment tend to attract the media's attention. The media can play a crucial role in disseminating information about the law, through news items, documentaries, educational programmes and specialist parenting magazines.

---

74. SIFO (1981), *Physical punishment and child abuse*, report of public opinion poll organisation in Sweden; also K.A. Ziegert (1983), "The Swedish prohibition of corporal punishment: a preliminary report", *Journal of Marriage and the Family*, November, pp. 917-926.

75. J. Staffan (2002), *op. cit.*, note 62.

Box 5 – Supporting law reform: educational measures

• Ensuring comprehensive awareness-raising of the prohibition of all corporal punishment and other inhuman or degrading treatment and humiliation of children, among children and all who live and work with them, and among the general public;

• Ensuring comprehensive awareness-raising of children's human rights, including the right to respect for their human dignity and physical integrity;

• Promoting positive, non-violent forms of child-rearing, conflict resolution and education to future parents, parents and other carers, and to the general public;

• Ensuring that children and young people have the opportunity to express their views and participate in planning and actions to eliminate corporal punishment;

• Ensuring that advice and appropriate support is available for all parents, and in particular for those who are finding child-rearing stressful;

• Ensuring that children have access to confidential advice and counselling as well as advocacy to challenge violence against them;

• Ensuring effective and appropriate forms of protection for children who may be particularly vulnerable to harmful and humiliating punishment – for example, children with disabilities;

• Ensuring that corporal punishment and other harmful and humiliating forms of discipline of children come within the definition of domestic or family violence and that strategies to eliminate punitive violence against children are built into strategies challenging domestic or family violence;

• Monitoring the effectiveness of abolition by regular research into children's experiences of violence in their homes, schools and other settings, and of child protection services and parents' experiences of and attitudes to violence against children.

In Sweden, the government started public education campaigns to discourage parental corporal punishment in the 1970s, but the campaign became large-scale as the explicit ban came into effect in 1979. It included an educational pamphlet, *Can you bring up children successfully without smacking and spanking?*, which was circulated to every household with children and to agencies in touch with families (see extracts below). The pamphlet includes a description of the law, and its history and motivation. One section emphasises the importance of parents setting limits and sticking to them – but also states that parents need to have an understanding of child development.

The media covered the law reform extensively. A short message explaining the law, with a cartoon of a small girl saying "I'll never ever hit my own children" was printed on milk cartons – often used as a vehicle for public information in Sweden. The law was promoted in parent education classes and child-health clinics.

Schools were targeted; for example, the law was used as an example in teaching children about the process of parliamentary law-making – so that they learnt about the content of the bill as well as about its passage through parliament. In English lessons, one of the materials was an audio-tape of a debate on corporal punishment, with an English man and woman defending its use.

Extracts – Can you bring up children successfully without smacking and spanking?

Why forbid all forms of physical punishment?

Psychologists, psychiatrists and other people whose work gives them insights into the parent-child relationship are practically unanimous in agreeing that all forms of physical punishment are highly objectionable as a method of bringing up children. A parent who strikes his or her child is not going to gain anything positive in the way of child education by this act – rather, the child runs the risk of suffering some form of mental harm.

The law therefore now forbids all forms of physical punishment of children, including smacking, etc., although it goes without saying that you can still snatch a child away from a hot stove or open window if there is a risk of its injuring itself.

Should physical punishment meted out to a child cause bodily injury or pain which is of more than very temporary duration it is classified as assault and is an offence punishable under the Criminal Code. In theory at least, this was also true before the new bill came into force, although it was not generally known. However, the advent of the new law has now swept all doubt aside, although as before trivial offences will remain unpunished, either because they cannot be classified as assault or because an action is not brought. But while the purpose of the new legislation is indeed to make it quite clear that spanking and beating are no longer allowed, it does not aim at having more parents punished than hitherto.

Many psychological punishments are at least as detrimental to a child's development as beating. Threatening, scaring or ostracising a child, locking it up or making it feel ridiculous can only be considered as injurious and humiliating treatment and are therefore forbidden.

Setting limits and sticking to them

Setting limits is absolutely necessary. However, before doing so parents should have a clear idea of exactly where they need to be set in view of the child's age and state of development. And furthermore, parents must be prepared to ask themselves why they consider these particular limits to be of importance. Limits felt to be justified should be closely observed and stuck to consistently – but it is still important that parents be aware of their own motives in setting them and that restrictions be made only after consideration of what is best for the child and its family.

Children need support and clearly defined bounds since this gives them a sense of security. Parents are endowed with a natural authority over their children since they have lived longer and have more experience. However, this is in no way the same as brandishing authority and making all the decisions without listening to the opinions of others. On the contrary, a relationship based on a continuous interplay with affectionate parents or guardians will gradually develop an inner voice within the child telling it what is allowed and what is not. This voice must not be weakened by the use of punishments.

Can one show anger?

Some people seem to make self-control and patience into a sort of code of honour; but if you have to strain yourself to bottle up your anger, disappointment or irritation you will also be running a great risk of keeping back feelings of genuine warmth and affection. Feelings don't all come out of separate taps, they come in a mixture. Parents obviously love their children a great deal but still get angry with them on occasions, so if you can admit to yourself your right to be angry it will be that much easier to avoid using bad methods such as physical punishments. Showing your distress and fear is much better.

Why was the law passed?

Because it is a natural historical development. We have already done away with the right to beat one's wife and servants. We have done away with the right to strike children at school.

Because our democratic community needs children taught to think for themselves, who are used to making their own choices and to shouldering responsibility. It is impossible to beat a child into obedience and at the same time expect it to be able to think for itself.

Because bringing up a child is much easier if you do not resort to beating. Children want to like you so very much that it is a pity to destroy a feeling of kinship and mutual understanding by beating if it can be avoided. You don't go round hitting your friends, do you? Why should you hit your children, then?

In Denmark, when the Danish Parliament adopted a law explicitly prohibiting corporal punishment and other humiliating treatment in 1997, it was accompanied by a government-supported campaign *Nej til bank* ("No to smacking"), launched by the National Council for Children, Children's Welfare and the government's Violence Secretariat. A mass-produced leaflet, *Parents do not have a right to hit their children*, translated into six languages, states that "Parents must raise their children without resorting to 'smacking'". It notes that in Denmark corporal punishment of prisoners was prohibited in 1911; in 1920 men were prohibited from beating wives and servants;

in 1967 school corporal punishment was prohibited – and finally in 1997 parents were prohibited from smacking their children.

Another leaflet, *When I have children, I will not smack them*, was sent to all parents with children up to 10 years of age, promoting positive forms of discipline. There were also posters and magazines with articles and advice. The leaflet suggests that parents who have questions about the law or want to discuss child-rearing can consult their health visitor, daycare staff, class teacher or general practitioner. Anonymous counselling is also available for parents.

In Germany, when explicit prohibition of corporal punishment was added to the Civil Code in 2000, the *Socialgesetzbuch*, the German child-care law, was amended to impose an active duty on local authorities to "promote ways in which families can resolve conflict without resort to force". One of the slogans that accompanied the legal change was "Help instead of punishment", emphasising that the aim was to change public opinion and support families in moving away from reliance on violent and negative forms of discipline.

Law reform was accompanied by a public education campaign, "More respect for children", funded by central government, but implemented by a combination of federal and local authorities and non-governmental organisations. The campaign varied from place to place owing to Germany's federal structure and used a wide range of methods to get the message across. These included slots on national television, leaflets and educational materials for parents, public events and workshops and structured "courses" as part of adult education. Continuing responsibility for the long-term implementation of the law has been passed to the federal and local authorities by the amendment to the child-care legislation mentioned above.

In other member states where legal reform is not yet complete or effective, non-governmental organisations have carried out major public- and parent-education campaigns to promote positive forms of discipline. Examples include Romania, where prohibition came into effect on 1 January 2005 (Save the Children Romania), Spain (Save the Children Spain) and Poland (Nobody's Children Foundation).

"Childhood without violence" – a campaign in Poland

The Nobody's Children Foundation in Poland, together with the State Agency for Solving Alcohol-related Problems and the Blue Line (a helpline for victims of domestic violence), developed a national campaign in 2001-2, aimed at reducing and preventing corporal punishment of children.[76]

The goals of the campaign were: social education about the consequences of using corporal punishment and of other forms of child abuse; the promotion of positive solutions for prevention, protection and intervention; improving support services for children and their families; and developing good parental skills and attitudes. The campaign targeted parents, the public, representatives of institutions and social services working with children, and local government.

At local level, "ambassadors" of the campaign organised debates and developed local programmes aimed at reducing the problem. The 354 ambassadors conducted more than 230 debates at district or municipality level, covering directly over 155 of Poland's communities. In addition, a media campaign was launched at national level (posters, billboards, TV commercials and two radio spots). Two months after the campaign ended, a follow-up study found that nearly two thirds (62%) of the respondents had noticed the campaign. Even more people (75%) had noticed messages or events that were part of the campaign, without necessarily knowing that a campaign was being conducted.

The Nobody's Children Foundation later prepared, at the request of the Council of Europe integrated project on "Responses to violence in everyday life in a democratic society", a handbook on how to raise awareness, primarily through campaigns to reduce corporal punishment, and how child abuse can be prevented.[77] The handbook presents case studies of three successful awareness-raising campaigns in

---

76. For details of the Nobody's Children Foundation, see <http://www.fdn.pl>.

77. M. Sajkowska and L. Wojtasik (2004), *Protecting children against corporal punishment – awareness campaigns*, Council of Europe Publishing.

the United Kingdom, Poland and the United States of America. The case studies describe how best to carry out such campaigns, and cover aspects such as working effectively with the media and pooling the work of the police, local authorities, teachers, parents and professionals. The handbook includes three useful model questionnaires aimed at support services, children and professionals.

Supporting parents and parenting

There can be no excuses for violence against children. Implementing law reform and public education to protect children cannot await better social conditions for families, any more than societies can wait for full employment and enhanced social conditions for men before challenging all domestic violence against women. But we need to acknowledge that poverty and inequality, poor housing and over-crowding, conflicts between insensitive employment policies and child-rearing, ill-health and other factors can all add to the stress of parenting.

So reducing violence against children is another motive for ensuring the social and economic rights of all Europe's citizens and above all for challenging poverty. The Council of Europe is currently addressing these issues by a new transversal action programme on "Children and violence" and also through the Committee of Experts on Children and Families (CS-EF) working in the framework of the Council of Europe Strategy for Social Cohesion. The committee has established two working parties – on children at risk of social exclusion and on parental skills, especially for preventing and combating violence affecting children.[78] In May 2006, the Conference of European Ministers Responsible for Family Affairs held its 28th Session in Lisbon, entitled "Changes in parenting: Children today, parents tomorrow". The CS-EF prepared the report "Parenting in contemporary Europe: a positive approach" as background material for the conference (see below).

---

78. The work of the Committee of Experts on Children and the Family can be followed at <http://www.coe.int/T/E/Social _ cohesion>.

A recommendation to member states was prepared and adopted by the Committee of Ministers on 13 December 2006 on policy to support positive parenting (see Appendix II). The recommendation calls on governments to "acknowledge the essential nature of families and of the parental role and create the necessary conditions for positive parenting in the best interests of the child [and] take all appropriate legislative, administrative, financial and other measures adhering to the principles" in the recommendation's appendix. The recommendation's explanatory report contains "key messages" for parents and guidelines for professionals.[79]

There are plans to produce guidelines on general topics related to positive parenting as well as specific situations, such as parenting of very young children or adolescents, children with disabilities, lone parents and reconstituted families.

Parenting in contemporary Europe – a positive approach

Parenting in contemporary Europe – a positive approach[80] focuses on parenting in contemporary European societies and develops a concept of positive parenting based on the child's best interests and taking into account the needs and resources of parents.

Based on an analytical review of documents relating to family law, parenting-related research reports, and medical and psychological research reports, *Parenting in contemporary Europe* offers a coherent and practical approach to positive parenting, founded on principles that advance the rights enunciated in the UN Convention on the Rights of the Child ("parenting in the vision of the UNCRC"), identified as nurturing, providing structure, giving recognition and enabling empowerment. For example, conditions that promote positive child behaviour include:

---

79. The explanatory report can be accessed via <http://www.coe.int> (Committee of Ministers, document A-Z index).

80. Council of Europe Publishing, Strasbourg, 2007.

- Maintaining a positive emotional tone in the home through play and parental warmth and affection for the child;

- Providing attention to the child to increase positive behaviour. For older children, attention includes being aware of and interested in school performance, other behaviour and peer contacts outside the home;

- Providing consistency in the form of regular times and patterns in daily activities and interactions to reduce resistance, convey respect for the child and make negative experiences less stressful;

- Responding consistently to similar behaviour situations to promote more harmonious parent-child relationships;

- Being flexible, particularly with older children and adolescents, through listening and negotiation to reduce episodes of child non-compliance with parental expectations. Involving the child in decision-making has been associated with long-term enhancement in moral judgment.

A number of strategies are suggested to help children learn positive behaviours:

- Providing regular positive attention and communicating this to children of all ages;

- Listening carefully to children and helping them to express their feelings;

- Helping children to learn how to evaluate the potential consequences of their choices;

- Reinforcing emerging desirable behaviours with frequent praise and ignoring trivial misdeeds;

- Modelling orderly, predictable behaviour, respectful communication and collaborative conflict-resolution strategies.

The report also includes an overview of some of the most common family-policy measures in European countries and explores elements of parenting support services and programmes.

In summarising, the report states:

> Parenting should aim to be nurturing, to provide the child with structure and limits, to give recognition and acknowledgement to the child and also to empower the child. In addition, parenting should be exercised in a non-violent manner, understanding violence as taking many forms. The how of parenting is therefore critical. It might help to make three points clear. First, we are not advocating permissive parenting – parents need to provide their children with structure and guidance. Nor is it a one-way street – parents should have expectations of their children and seek to be consistent in this respect. Secondly, we emphasise the value of change and progression. One of the main foundations of the UNCRC is the idea of the evolving capacities of the child. In other words, parenting practices must be progressive in the sense of changing as the child gets older. Thirdly, we emphasise that parents are not or should not be alone with their responsibilities. It is our view, and indeed also the view underlying the UNCRC, that states parties have the responsibility to ensure that parents have access to the necessary resources and conditions to enable them to exercise their parenting role in a positive manner.

Advice, counselling and advocacy services for children

Children need to know where they can go for advice and help about things that concern them, including violence against them in the family. Several countries have confidential free telephone advice and counselling services for children. But it seems there has been little serious consideration in most states of how children can seek realistic remedies for breaches of their rights, including the right to be protected from all forms of violence within the family.

In Sweden, research commissioned by the Parliamentary Committee on Child Abuse and Related Issues in 2001 found that one third of children exposed to corporal punishment before their teens reported that they had no person whom they could trust, to whom they could turn for comfort or in whom they could confide.[81] In all countries, there are social services, the police and others to whom children can go to report violence. But inevitably, children are only going to use these services if they have confidence that any action and intervention that may follow will be sensitive to their status and genuinely in their best interests.

Integrating the ending of corporal punishment into strategies to challenge domestic or family violence

Recommendations to member states from the Council of Europe's Committee of Ministers have emphasised that ending corporal punishment is an essential part of challenging domestic or family violence. The definition of domestic violence in some member states focuses exclusively on violence between adult family members, primarily violence against women. It may encompass the effect on children of witnessing violence between adults, but it does not invariably include direct violence by adults against children in the domestic setting.

The concept of "zero tolerance" of domestic violence against women has not been extended consistently to apply to all corporal punishment of children. While there is a need for awareness-raising programmes – and special legal and other strategies – to eliminate violence between adult partners, it is essential that they should not condone, directly or indirectly, violence against children. Definitions and programmes in the field of domestic or family violence should be reviewed to ensure that they promote an end to all corporal punishment and deliberate humiliation of children.

More broadly, ending corporal punishment needs to be integrated into strategies to prevent all forms of violence, including bullying and other forms of violence between children, which tend to have their roots in adult violence against children.

---

81. J. Staffan (2002), *op. cit.*, note 62.

Monitoring the effectiveness of protection

As indicated in Chapter 3, research into children's experiences of violence, in particular within the family, is still rare in member states. The only way to survey the effectiveness of law reform and accompanying educational measures is to carry out regular confidential interview research with parents and children. These interviews can be used to monitor all forms of violence experienced by children, not only in the family, but in their schools, other institutions, on the streets and in their communities. The methodology for this research exists in a number of countries, but needs to be applied in all countries and at regular intervals.

Sweden's Parliamentary Committee on Child Abuse and Related Issues, in its final report issued in 2001, proposed that Statistics Sweden should be commissioned to survey every three years pupils' experiences of violence in the home, at school and in leisure activities: "In our view, knowledge of children's and adolescents' own experiences and perceptions of abuse and other forms of maltreatment should be used in both preventive and remedial work." In addition, the committee proposed that surveys be carried out every three years of parents' experiences of, and attitudes to, violence against their own children.[82]

---

82. Parliamentary Committee on Child Abuse and Related Issues (2001), *Child abuse – prevention and protection, English summary of final report*, Ministry of Health and Social Affairs, Sweden.

Selected reading – learn more

Council of Europe

Parenting in contemporary Europe – a positive approach: Council of Europe Publishing, Strasbourg, 2007.

Protecting children from corporal punishment – awareness-raising campaigns: Council of Europe Publishing, Strasbourg, 2004.

Views on positive parenting and non-violent upbringing: Council of Europe Publishing, Strasbourg, 2007.

Websites

Building a Europe for and with children – a Council of Europe programme: <http://www.coe.int/children>.

Council of Europe home page: <http://www.coe.int>, provides access to: the Committee of Ministers, the European Court of Human Rights, the European Social Charter (via human rights activities), the Commissioner for Human Rights.

"The right not to be hit – also a children's right", Thomas Hammarberg, Council of Europe Commissioner for Human Rights: <http://www. coe.int/children> (speeches/Hammarberg).

Other sources

Eliminating corporal punishment: the way forward to constructive child discipline, ed. Stuart N. Hart: Unesco Publishing, 2005.

Ending corporal punishment: Swedish experience of efforts to prevent all forms of violence against children – and the results: Ministry of Health and Social Affairs and Ministry of Foreign Affairs, Sweden, 2001.

Implementation handbook for the Convention on the Rights of the Child, fully revised 2nd edition (includes detailed analysis of the developing jurisprudence of the Committee on the Rights of the Child): Unicef, 2002 (a 3rd edition is forthcoming in 2007).

It hurts you inside – children talking about smacking, Carolyne Willow and Tina Hyder: National Children's Bureau and Save the Children, London, 1998.

Global Initiative to End All Corporal Punishment of Children: <http://www.endcorporalpunishment.org>;
(e-mail: info@endcorporalpunishment.org>.

World report on violence against children: United Nations, Geneva, 2006.

Appendices

I.
Parliamentary Assembly Recommendation 1666 (2004)[83] on a Europe-wide ban on corporal punishment of children

1. The Parliamentary Assembly notes that, according to the European Committee of Social Rights, in order to comply with the European Social Charter and the revised European Social Charter, member states must ban all forms of corporal punishment and any other forms of degrading punishment or treatment of children. Five member states fail to meet these requirements because they have not effectively prohibited all forms of corporal punishment. A collective complaints procedure has been lodged against five other member states on the same grounds.

2. The Assembly also notes that the European Court of Human Rights has found in successive judgments that corporal punishment violates children's rights as guaranteed under the European Convention on Human Rights. These decisions applied initially to corporal punishment in young offenders' institutions, then in schools, including private schools, and most recently within the family. Moreover, both the European Commission of Human Rights until 1998 and the Court have emphasised that banning all corporal punishment does not breach the right to private or family life or religious freedom.

3. The Assembly observes that all member states have ratified the United Nations Convention on the Rights of the Child, which requires them to protect children from all forms of physical or mental violence by adults while in their care. The Committee on the Rights of the Child, which monitors compliance with the Convention, has

---

83. *Assembly debate* on 23 June 2004 (21st Sitting) (see Doc.10199, report of the Social, Health and Family Affairs Committee, rapporteur: Ms Bargholtz). *Text adopted by the Assembly* on 23 June 2004 (21st Sitting).

consistently interpreted the latter as requiring member states both to prohibit all forms of corporal punishment of children and to educate and inform the public on the subject.

4. The Assembly welcomes the current global initiative to end all corporal punishment of children and wishes to add its support to that already given by Unicef, Unesco, the United Nations High Commissioner for Human Rights, the Commissioner for Human Rights of the Council of Europe, the European Network of Ombudsmen for Children (ENOC) and numerous national and international human rights institutions and non-governmental organisations across Europe.

5. The Assembly considers that any corporal punishment of children is in breach of their fundamental right to human dignity and physical integrity. The fact that such corporal punishment is still lawful in certain member states violates their equally fundamental right to the same legal protection as adults. Striking a human being is prohibited in European society and children are human beings. The social and legal acceptance of corporal punishment of children must be ended.

6. The Assembly is concerned to note that, so far, only a minority of the forty-five member states has formally prohibited corporal punishment in the family and in all other contexts. While they have all banned corporal punishment in schools, including private schools and other educational institutions, this does not necessarily extend to residential and all other forms of childcare. Nor are such bans systematically and universally respected.

7. The Assembly therefore invites the Council of Europe's Committee of Ministers to launch a co-ordinated and concerted campaign in all the member states for the total abolition of corporal punishment of children. The Assembly notes the success of the Council of Europe in abolishing the death penalty and the Assembly now calls on the Organisation to work in the same way to make Europe, as soon as possible, a corporal punishment-free zone for children.

8. It invites the Committee of Ministers and the other Council of Europe bodies concerned, as a matter of urgency, to establish strategies, including technical assistance, for achieving this objective in conjunction with member states, and in particular to:

i. heighten the awareness of children, those who live and work with them and the general public of the total ban on corporal punishment and other forms of humiliating, inhuman and degrading treatment of children;

ii. ensure general awareness of children's fundamental rights, in particular their right to human dignity and physical integrity;

iii. encourage positive, non-violent forms of child-rearing and conflict resolution among future and existing parents, all other people who care for children as well as the public at large;

iv. offer children and young people the opportunity to express their views and be involved in planning and implementing activities to eradicate corporal punishment;

v. make sure that parents, particularly those experiencing difficulties with child-rearing, are offered the necessary advice and support;

vi. offer children confidential advice, counselling and legal representation so that they can respond to violence against them;

vii. guarantee effective and appropriate protection to children who are particularly vulnerable to harmful and humiliating punishment, such as disabled children and children in institutions or detention facilities;

viii. ensure that corporal punishment and other harmful and humiliating forms of discipline inflicted on children are included in the definition of domestic or family violence and that strategies to combat the violent punishment of children form an integral part of strategies against domestic or family violence.

9. Finally, the Assembly invites the Committee of Ministers to recommend that the member states:

i. enact appropriate legislation prohibiting the corporal punishment of children, particularly within the family;

ii. monitor the effectiveness of abolition through regular research into children's experience of violence at home, in school and elsewhere, the effectiveness of child protection services and parents' experience of and attitudes to violence against children;

iii. ensure that the relevant judgments of the European Court of Human Rights and the conclusions of the European Committee of Social Rights are fully applied.

II.
Recommendation Rec(2006)19 of the Committee of Ministers to member states on policy to support positive parenting

(Adopted by the Committee of Ministers on 13 December 2006 at the 983rd meeting of the Ministers' Deputies)

The Committee of Ministers, under Article 15.*b* of the Statute of the Council of Europe,

Considering that the aim of the Council of Europe is to achieve a greater unity between its member states, *inter alia*, by promoting the adoption of common rules;

Referring to the work of the Council of Europe in the field of children and families and reaffirming in general the following legal instruments:

- the Convention on Human Rights and Fundamental Freedoms (ETS No. 5), which protects the rights of everyone, including children;

- the European Social Charter (ETS No. 35) and revised European Social Charter (ETS No. 163), stating that "the family as a fundamental unit of society has the right to appropriate social, legal and economic protection to ensure its full development" (Article 16);

- the European Convention on the Exercise of Children's Rights (ETS No. 160);

- the Convention on Contacts concerning children (ETS No. 192);

- the Recommendations of the Committee of Ministers to member states: No. R (84) 4 on parental responsibilities; No. R (85) 4 on violence in the family; No. R (87) 6 on foster families; No. R (94) 14 on coherent and integrated family policies; No. R (96) 5 on reconciling work and family life; No. R (97) 4 on securing and promoting the health of single parent families; No. R (98) 8 on children's participation in family and social life; Rec(2005)5 on the rights of children living in residential institutions and Rec(2006)5 on the Council of Europe Action Plan to promote the rights and full participation of people with disabilities in society: improving the quality of life of people with disabilities in Europe 2006-2015;

Bearing in mind the Revised Social Strategy for Social Cohesion for which families are the place where social cohesion is first experienced and learnt and that a social cohesion strategy, while fully respecting the autonomy of the private sphere and of civil society, must seek to be supportive of families;

Recalling the Parliamentary Assembly's Recommendations 751 (1975) on the position and responsibility of parents in the modern family and their support by society; 1074 (1988) on family policy; 1121 (1990) on the rights of children; 1443 (2000) on international adoption: respecting children's rights; 1501 (2001) on parents' and teachers' responsibilities in children's education; 1551 (2002) on building a 21st-century society with and for children: follow-up to the European strategy for children (Recommendation 1286 (1996)); 1639 (2003) on family mediation and equality of sexes; 1666 (2004) on a Europe-wide ban on corporal punishment of children; 1698 (2005) on the rights of children in institutions: follow-up to Recommendation 1601 (2003) of the Parliamentary Assembly;

Stressing the importance of the United Nations Convention on the Rights of the Child, to which all the member states of the Council of Europe are Parties, and the basic principles of which should always underlie the rearing of children;

Recalling the Third Summit of Heads of State and Government (Warsaw, Poland, May 2005) and the commitment made there to fully comply with the obligations of the United Nations Convention on the Rights of the Child, to effectively promote the rights of the child and to take specific action to eradicate all forms of violence against children, and the ensuing programme "Building a Europe for and with children", officially launched in Monaco, on 4 and 5 April 2006;

Referring to the Final Communiqué and Political Declaration of the European Ministers responsible for Family Affairs at their 28th session (Lisbon, Portugal, 16-17 May 2006), particularly:

- recognising that parenting, though linked to family intimacy, should be designated as a domain of public policy and all the necessary measures should be adopted for supporting parenting and creating the conditions necessary for positive parenting;

- recalling their commitment to promote and pursue a common European policy in the field of family affairs and the rights of the child within the framework of the Council of Europe;

Recognising the child as a person with rights, including the right to be protected and to participate, to express her/his views, to be heard and be heeded;

Recalling that public authorities have a vital role to play in supporting families in general and parents in particular, which is expressed through three core elements of family policy: public transfers and taxation, measures to balance work and family life, childcare provision and other services;

Considering that the family is a primary unit of society and that parenting plays a fundamental role in society and for its future;

Conscious of the many changes and challenges facing families today which require parenthood to be given greater prominence and better support, considering that such support is essential for children, parents and society as a whole;

Recognising that all levels of society have a role to play in supporting children, parents and families;

Considering that public authorities in conjunction with the economic and social sectors and civil society can, in taking action in support of parenting, help strive for a healthier and more prosperous future for society, as well as an improvement in the quality of family life;

Noting the need for a cross-sectoral and co-ordinated approach;

Keen to promote positive parenting as an essential part of the support provided for parenting, and as a means of ensuring respect for and implementation of children's rights,

Recommends that the governments of member states:

- acknowledge the essential nature of families and of the parental role and create the necessary conditions for positive parenting in the best interests of the child;

- take all appropriate legislative, administrative, financial and other measures adhering to the principles set out in the appendix to this recommendation.

Appendix to the Recommendation Rec(2006)19

1.   Definitions

For the purpose of this recommendation, the term:

"Parents": refers to persons with parental authority or responsibility;

"Parenting": refers to all the roles falling to parents in order to care for and bring up children. Parenting is centred on parent-children interaction and entails rights and duties for the child's development and self-fulfilment;

"Positive parenting": refers to parental behaviour based on the best interests of the child that is nurturing, empowering, non-violent and provides recognition and guidance which involves setting of boundaries to enable the full development of the child.

2. Fundamental principles of policies and measures

Policies and measures in the field of support for parenting should:

i. adopt a rights-based approach: this means treating children and parents as holders of rights and obligations;

ii. be based on a voluntary choice by the individuals concerned, except when public authorities have to intervene to protect the child;

iii. acknowledge that parents have the prime responsibility for their child, subject to the child's best interests;

iv. consider parents and children as partners sharing, as appropriate, the setting up and implementation of the measures relating to them;

v. be based on the equal involvement of parents and respect for their complementarity;

vi. guarantee equal opportunities for children irrespective of their gender, status, abilities or family situation;

vii. take into account the importance of a sufficient standard of living to engage in positive parenting;

viii. be based on a clearly expressed concept of positive parenting;

ix. address parents and key players having childcare, health and educational and social responsibilities towards the child and who should also respect the principles of positive parenting;

x. recognise the diverse types of parenting and parental situations through adopting a pluralistic approach;

xi. adopt a positive approach to parents' potential, particularly through placing priority on incentives;

xii.   be long-term in order to guarantee stability and continuity of policy;

xiii. ensure that the number of common rules of principle at national or federal level are kept to a minimum to promote equal standards at local level and that there is a local network of services providing parenting support measures;

xiv.   ensure inter-ministerial co-operation, encouraging and co-ordinating the action(s) in this field of the different ministries, departments and agencies concerned in order to implement policy that is coherent and comprehensive;

xv.   be co-ordinated at international level, through facilitating exchanges of knowledge, experience and good practice in the application of the guidelines on positive parenting.

3.   Objectives

Governments should organise their policies and programmes on positive parenting with a view to achieving the following three types of objectives:

i.   the creation of the conditions for positive parenting, by ensuring that all those rearing children have access to an appropriate level and diversity of resources (material, psychological, social and cultural) and that broad social attitudes and patterns of prevailing life are receptive to the needs of families with children and also those of parents;

ii.   the removal of barriers to positive parenting, whatever their origin. Employment policy, in particular, should allow a better reconciliation of family and working life;

iii.   the promotion of positive parenting by developing awareness of it and taking all the necessary measures to make it a reality. In order to have efficient policies to support parenting, public authorities should promote initiatives aiming to make people aware of the value and importance of positive parenting.

Governments should take a pro-active approach to promoting awareness of parenting issues and to normalising participation in parenting programmes. Information should present different images of parenting in order to avoid stigmatising differences.

The goal of policy and measures should be the harmonious development (in all its dimensions) and proper treatment of children, with due regard for their fundamental rights and dignity. As a priority, measures should be taken to eliminate all child neglect and abuse and physical or psychological violence (including humiliation, degrading treatment and corporal punishment).

It is also essential to implement and further develop a suitable policy to bring about a change in social attitudes and patterns of life in order to accommodate more effectively the needs of children, parents and families and in particular to promote family-friendly working environments and services.

4.   Incorporating children's rights in public policies

Public policies on support for parenting should incorporate childhood-related issues, acknowledging the needs and interests of all children and paying attention to their varying needs depending on their age, capacity, and level of maturity. For this purpose, the principles enshrined in the United Nations Convention on the Rights of the Child should be respected by all, regardless of context, and particularly guide the activities of all bodies working in the field, both public and private, especially for the following rights and general principles:

i.   the right to non-discrimination;

ii.   the best interests of the child should be of primary consideration;

iii.   the child's right to life and development;

ix.   the child's right to participation, to express her/his views, to be heard and be heeded, to receive information and to join associations and other organisations;

x.   the right to protection and care.

For this purpose, it is important for the child to grow up in a favourable family environment and in a positive atmosphere.

5.   Considering parents' responsibilities, rights and obligations

In the best interests of the child, the rights of parents, such as entitlement to appropriate support from public authorities in fulfilling their parental functions, must also be given prominence. The exercise by parents of equal and shared responsibility for their children makes a major contribution to the harmonious development of the child's personality.

Particular attention should be paid to the important role of fathers in the care and rearing of their children, taking into account in particular the principle of gender equality, the impact on families of the reconciliation of work and family life and family breakdown, which can often result in fathers living apart from their children.

6.   Core components of policies and measures

Policies to promote and encourage positive parenting will work best if they are based on consultation and dialogue with parents and on their voluntary involvement and participation, in order to reach a real partnership. In addition to the essential elements at point 4 and 5 of this recommendation, core components include the following:

6.1.   Supporting parents

i.   alongside the measures proposed by public authorities to afford and improve support for parents, support from other agencies (such as municipalities, social security and associations) should also be acknowledged and encouraged;

ii.   policies should be geared to engendering support for parenting at the following three levels:

- informal: creating and strengthening existing social bonds and encouraging new links between parents and their family, neighbours and friends;

- semi-formal: empowering parents' and children's associations and NGOs and activating a range of self-help and other community-based groups and services;

- formal: facilitating access to public services.

6.2. *Promoting education in children's rights and positive parenting*

i.   parents should be encouraged to become more aware of the nature of their role (and how it is changing), children's rights, the responsibilities and obligations that derive from these and their own rights;

ii.   governments should also arrange for comprehensive guidelines and specific programmes to assist them in challenging life situations, conflict resolution, anger management through non-violent approaches and mediation techniques;

iii.   prevention programmes regarding the different forms of ill-treatment of children should be promoted and parents made aware of this serious problem and of its consequences on the child's development;

iv.   children should also be taught about their rights and duties in order to make them aware of the concept of positive parenting and what this means for them.

6.3. *Reconciling family and working life*

i.   public authorities should create the necessary conditions – and employers should be encouraged – to implement a better reconciliation of family and working life through legal and other provisions (such as flexible working arrangements, adjustment of working and school hours, leave policies, various types of good quality childcare services, provisions for looking after children with disabilities as well as sick children, etc.);

ii.   the social partners should be encouraged to negotiate and develop tailor-made policies adapted to the specific needs of each company and of their employees;

iii.   good practices make it clear to employers that a comprehensive work/life balance policy creates a win-win situation within companies.

6.4.   Policies at local level

The action taken at local level is particularly important in providing a response tailored more closely to the needs and characteristics of the populations concerned. Co-operation and co-ordination at national or federal and local levels and between these levels are necessary in order to offer families better service and optimise available resources and the use made of them. Administrative procedures should allow for an appropriate level of flexibility in service provision, consistent with ensuring equitable treatment of all families.

7.   Targeting of policies and measures

Particular attention should be paid to difficult social and economic circumstances and to crises within families, which require more specific support.

It is also essential to supplement general policies with a more targeted approach. Parenting in certain situations and at certain periods in the life cycle is by its nature more challenging. Despite the variations from country to country, the needs of the following groups should be especially attended to:

i.   first-time parents;

ii.   teenage parents;

iii.   families with particular needs;

iv.   families in difficult socio-economic circumstances.

In the case of separated parents, support policies should be aimed in particular at maintaining links between children and both their parents, unless this is contrary to the child's best interests. Access to professional counselling should be provided and attention should be paid to cases where the parents have different cultural backgrounds or are of different nationalities.

Public authorities should stimulate and facilitate the creation of networks of mutual assistance associations between families and make available places where parents could meet to discuss – with professionals, if necessary – on issues relating to parenting, and provide parents with adequate support services like free help lines and counselling services.

8. Parenting in situations of social exclusion

Parenting in situations of social exclusion or at risk of social exclusion can be particularly difficult and special attention should be paid to the needs of children and families in this situation, with reference in particular to the following:

i. providing long-term support, as appropriate, to help them achieve the same results as other children and families; this support should include reaching out to them in their homes or in the places they frequent, and take into consideration the possible fear of parents in a situation of social exclusion towards social services, particularly of having their children taken away;

ii. giving sufficient means to support parents and to allow them to acquire the necessary competence to fulfil their responsibilities towards their children;

iii. guaranteeing access to social rights (including the right to adequate income, health, education, housing and employment) and the same quality targeted services as those enjoyed by other families;

iv. ensuring that families and children suffering exclusion are considered in their social context (including the extended family, the community and their relational networks) and enjoy the same quality services, including local ones, as those enjoyed by other families, in accordance with their needs;

v. building a trustworthy relationship with the families and enabling parents to regain control of their own lives;

vi. organising training for professionals and parents together in order to achieve better mutual knowledge and understanding, to build a common project in the best interests of the child and enabling professionals to learn about what these families are experiencing and to better know their family project, with a view to focusing their practice on it;

vii. ensuring personal and collective support for professionals in order to raise their level of competence in working with people in very difficult situations and take the necessary steps to create new approaches;

viii. taking ad hoc measures to avoid the risk of marginalisation of migrant families;

ix. avoiding measures and administrative practice that stigmatise children and parents by treating them differently because their families are less well-off than others;

x. introducing measures to prevent dropout from school as an efficient means to counteract family distress.

9. Qualitative guidelines for professionals

In order for the above rights and principles to be applied, benchmarks and standards must be set. Guidelines on the focus of their services – such as the Council of Europe guidelines on positive parenting – should be given to professionals and practitioners (including those not directly involved with children but whose work could have an impact on their rights), with particular emphasis on:

i. the principle of equity and accessibility, which should underlie all action taken;

ii. the principle of becoming partners with and empowering parents. Partnership presupposes recognition of parents' own experience and their knowledge of their own children;

iii. application of the concept of partnership to co-operation and interdisciplinary co-ordination between agencies, specifying the particular areas of activity of each department, providing for a sharing of facilities and working in a cross-curricular network;

iv. ensuring that the application of comprehensive services is conceived in terms of support and assistance, encouraging family initiative without creating excessive dependency. Accordingly, strengths and resources of families should be supported. This also means that professionals should act as support for parents, in ways that are non-judgmental and non-stigmatising;

v. building up parents' self-confidence, enhancing their competencies and potential and motivating parents to be informed and trained;

vi. enabling children to communicate their feelings and needs, in particular very young children and children with communication impairments;

vii. the importance of service provision and professional practices by ensuring that the emphasis is placed on:

- thorough training of the professionals concerned;

- ongoing evaluation, both external and internal (self-evaluation);

- continuity of action;

- responses based on the understanding of the child and families in their context;

viii. devising methods to identify risk factors regarding failure to provide parental care to be disseminated among social services, health-care professionals, those dealing with young people, teachers and childcare staff to train them in identifying families with problems in this respect and offer support. A better co-ordination among the services working to support a family should constantly be sought;

ix. co-ordinating the implementation of measures to separate children from their parents, when this is necessary, with work with the family of origin (particularly in partnership with the parents) in order to enable them to prepare or better prepare for and accept this step as a means of ensuring the best interests of the child. The aim of any such measure should be the return, if possible, of the child in the family environment.

10. School and childcare environment

An integrated approach to the provision of assistance with schooling and support for parenting should be encouraged (especially where children lack stable roots or a permanent home – for example children with a Roma or Gypsy background, children of migrants); childcare and school integration as well as dialogue between these service providers and parents should be encouraged, with special attention to families in difficult situations and to those with particular needs.

11. Key messages for parents and all those having responsibilities for children and their rearing

Key messages on positive parenting should be issued to all parents and persons providing care and involved in the rearing of a child on a daily basis (such as childminders or school staff). These messages should make clear how the child is to be respected as a person and how his/her participation should be promoted, and that parents have rights as well as responsibilities. Key messages should be drawn up on the basis of consultation with all the stakeholders involved, especially parents, service providers and children, and be monitored to ensure that they are effective and are being adhered to.

12. International co-operation

Measures should be put in place to improve international co-operation and exchange of best practice in relation to parenting.

III.
General observation of the European Committee of Social Rights – extract

Whereas the committee has not previously criticised any Contracting Party for not clearly prohibiting corporal punishment of children, it has requested information about legislation and practice in the Contracting Parties in particular as regards the protection of children against ill-treatment, with a view to re-examine the implementation of Article 17, in the light of national legislation and international conventions. While examining national situations, the committee has observed that the UN Committee encourages countries to reform their legislation with a view to ensuring the prohibition of corporal punishment inter alia within the family,[84] which is in line with the relevant provision in the Convention on the Rights of the Child.[85]

It has also observed that the European Court of Human Rights has held in a case[86] where a young boy was beaten by his stepfather, who pleaded that the treatment in question amounted to "reasonable chastisement", that it was of sufficient severity to fall under the scope of Article 3 of the European Convention on Human Rights. The Court considered that the obligation on the High Contracting Parties under Article 1 of the Convention to secure to everyone within their jurisdiction the rights and freedoms defined in the Convention, taken together with Article 3, required states to take measures designed to ensure that individuals within their jurisdiction are not subjected to

---

84. CRC/C/15/Add.38 (Concluding Observations/Comments), para. 15.

85. Article 19, para. 1, provides: "States Parties shall take all appropriate legislative, administrative, social and educational measures to protect the child from all forms of physical or mental violence, injury or abuse, neglect or negligent treatment, maltreatment or exploitation, including sexual abuse, while in the care of parent(s), legal guardian(s) or any other person who has the care of the child."

86. Judgment of 23 September 1998 in the case of *A v. UK*, para. 22.

torture or inhuman or degrading treatment or punishment, including such ill-treatment administered by private individuals. It stated that "children and other vulnerable individuals, in particular, are entitled to state protection, in the form of effective deterrence, against such serious breaches of personal integrity (see, *mutatis mutandis*, the *X and Y v. Netherlands* judgment of 26 March 1985, Series A no. 91, pp. 11–13, §§ 21–27; the *Stubbings and Others v. UK* judgment of 22 October 1996, *Reports* 1996-IV, p. 1505, §§ 62–64; and also the UN Convention on the Rights of the Child, Articles 19 and 37)".

The committee attaches great importance to the protection of children against any form of violence, ill-treatment or abuse, whether physical or mental. Like the European Court of Human Rights it emphasises the fact that children are particularly vulnerable and considers that one of the main objectives of Article 17 is to provide adequate protection for children in this respect.

The committee observes that in the last decades corporal punishment of children has been explicitly prohibited by law in several Contracting Parties.[87] It observes that Recommendation No. R (90) 2 on social measures concerning violence within the family adopted by the Committee of Ministers on 15 January 1990 in its Appendix, point 14 emphasises the general condemnation of corporal punishment and other forms of degrading treatment as a means of education.

The committee does not find it acceptable that a society which prohibits any form of physical violence between adults would accept that adults subject children to physical violence. The committee does not consider that there can be any educational value in corporal punishment of children that cannot be otherwise achieved.

Moreover, in a field where the available statistics show a constant increase in the number of cases of ill-treatment of children reported to the police and prosecutors, it is evident that additional measures to come to terms with this problem are necessary. To prohibit any form of corporal punishment of children is an important measure for

87. Namely: Austria, Denmark, Finland, Iceland, Norway and Sweden.

the education of the population in this respect in that it gives a clear message about what society considers to be acceptable.[88] It is a measure that avoids discussions and concerns as to where the borderline would be between what might be acceptable corporal punishment and what is not.

For these reasons, the committee considers that Article 17 requires a prohibition in legislation against any form of violence against children, whether at school, in other institutions, in their home or elsewhere. It furthermore considers that any other form of degrading punishment or treatment of children must be prohibited in legislation and combined with adequate sanctions in penal or civil law.

---

88. According to a survey made by the Central Office for Statistics in Sweden in 1996, 90% of the adult population supported the 1979 prohibition against corporal punishment of children. Source: *Are children protected against violence in Europe? An initial comparative study on laws, policies and practices in the European Union*, European Forum for Child Welfare, p. 98.

Building a Europe for and with children – publications

Abolishing corporal punishment of children – Questions and answers (2007)

Highlights (Monaco Conference) 2007

The Internet literacy handbook (2006)
ISBN 978-92-871-6099-7
(Also available in Russian)

Violence reduction in schools – how to make a difference (2006)
ISBN 978-92-871-5870-3
(Also available in Russian)

The Council of Europe programme "Building a Europe for and with children" was launched to promote and secure respect for children's rights in Europe, and protect children from all forms of violence. To learn more, visit www.coe.int/children.

ISBN titles may be ordered from: Council of Europe Publishing, http://book.coe.int
For others, contact: children@coe.int

Sales agents for publications of the Council of Europe
Agents de vente des publications du Conseil de l'Europe

BELGIUM/BELGIQUE
La Librairie Européenne -
The European Bookshop
Rue de l'Orme, 1
B-1040 BRUXELLES
Tel.: +32 (0)2 231 04 35
Fax: +32 (0)2 735 08 60
E-mail: order@libeurop.be
http://www.libeurop.be

Jean De Lannoy
Avenue du Roi 202 Koningslaan
B-1190 BRUXELLES
Tel.: +32 (0)2 538 43 08
Fax: +32 (0)2 538 08 41
E-mail: jean.de.lannoy@dl-servi.com
http://www.jean-de-lannoy.be

CANADA
Renouf Publishing Co. Ltd.
1-5369 Canotek Road
OTTAWA, Ontario K1J 9J3, Canada
Tel.: +1 613 745 2665
Fax: +1 613 745 7660
Toll-Free Tel.: (866) 767-6766
E-mail: order.dept@renoufbooks.com
http://www.renoufbooks.com

CZECH REPUBLIC/
RÉPUBLIQUE TCHÈQUE
Suweco CZ, s.r.o.
Klecakova 347
CZ-180 21 PRAHA 9
Tel.: +420 2 424 59 204
Fax: +420 2 848 21 646
E-mail: import@suweco.cz
http://www.suweco.cz

DENMARK/DANEMARK
GAD
Vimmelskaftet 32
DK-1161 KØBENHAVN K
Tel.: +45 77 66 60 00
Fax: +45 77 66 60 01
E-mail: gad@gad.dk
http://www.gad.dk

FINLAND/FINLANDE
Akateeminen Kirjakauppa
PO Box 128
Keskuskatu 1
FIN-00100 HELSINKI
Tel.: +358 (0)9 121 4430
Fax: +358 (0)9 121 4242
E-mail: akatilaus@akateeminen.com
http://www.akateeminen.com

FRANCE
La Documentation française
(diffusion/distribution France entière)
124, rue Henri Barbusse
F-93308 AUBERVILLIERS CEDEX
Tél.: +33 (0)1 40 15 70 00
Fax: +33 (0)1 40 15 68 00
E-mail: commande@ladocumentationfrancaise.fr
http://www.ladocumentationfrancaise.fr

Librairie Kléber
1 rue des Francs Bourgeois
F-67000 STRASBOURG
Tel.: +33 (0)3 88 15 78 88
Fax: +33 (0)3 88 15 78 80
E-mail: francois.wolfermann@librairie-kleber.fr
http://www.librairie-kleber.com

GERMANY/ALLEMAGNE
AUSTRIA/AUTRICHE
UNO Verlag GmbH
August-Bebel-Allee 6
D-53175 BONN
Tel.: +49 (0)228 94 90 20
Fax: +49 (0)228 94 90 222
E-mail: bestellung@uno-verlag.de
http://www.uno-verlag.de

GREECE/GRÈCE
Librairie Kauffmann s.a.
Stadiou 28
GR-105 64 ATHINAI
Tel.: +30 210 32 55 321
Fax: +30 210 32 30 320
E-mail: ord@otenet.gr
http://www.kauffmann.gr

HUNGARY/HONGRIE
Euro Info Service kft.
1137 Bp. Szent István krt. 12.
H-1137 BUDAPEST
Tel.: +36 (06)1 329 2170
Fax: +36 (06)1 349 2053
E-mail: euroinfo@euroinfo.hu
http://www.euroinfo.hu

ITALY/ITALIE
Licosa SpA
Via Duca di Calabria, 1/1
I-50125 FIRENZE
Tel.: +39 0556 483215
Fax: +39 0556 41257
E-mail: licosa@licosa.com
http://www.licosa.com

MEXICO/MEXIQUE
Mundi-Prensa México, S.A. De C.V.
Río Pánuco, 141 Delegación Cuauhtémoc
06500 MÉXICO, D.F.
Tel.: +52 (01)55 55 33 56 58
Fax: +52 (01)55 55 14 67 99
E-mail: mundiprensa@mundiprensa.com.mx
http://www.mundiprensa.com.mx

NETHERLANDS/PAYS-BAS
De Lindeboom Internationale Publicaties b.v.
M.A. de Ruyterstraat 20 A
NL-7482 BZ HAAKSBERGEN
Tel.: +31 (0)53 5740004
Fax: +31 (0)53 5729296
E-mail: books@delindeboom.com
http://www.delindeboom.com

NORWAY/NORVÈGE
Akademika
Postboks 84 Blindern
N-0314 OSLO
Tel.: +47 2 218 8100
Fax: +47 2 218 8103
E-mail: support@akademika.no
http://www.akademika.no

POLAND/POLOGNE
Ars Polona JSC
25 Obroncow Street
PL-03-933 WARSZAWA
Tel.: +48 (0)22 509 86 00
Fax: +48 (0)22 509 86 10
E-mail: arspolona@arspolona.com.pl
http://www.arspolona.com.pl

PORTUGAL
Livraria Portugal
(Dias & Andrade, Lda.)
Rua do Carmo, 70
P-1200-094 LISBOA
Tel.: +351 21 347 42 82 / 85
Fax: +351 21 347 02 64
E-mail: info@livrariaportugal.pt
http://www.livrariaportugal.pt

RUSSIAN FEDERATION/
FÉDÉRATION DE RUSSIE
Ves Mir
9a, Kolpacnhyi per.
RU-101000 MOSCOW
Tel.: +7 (8)495 623 6839
Fax: +7 (8)495 625 4269
E-mail: orders@vesmirbooks.ru
http://www.vesmirbooks.ru

SPAIN/ESPAGNE
Mundi-Prensa Libros, s.a.
Castelló, 37
E-28001 MADRID
Tel.: +34 914 36 37 00
Fax: +34 915 75 39 98
E-mail: libreria@mundiprensa.es
http://www.mundiprensa.com

SWITZERLAND/SUISSE
Van Diermen Editions – ADECO
Chemin du Lacuez 41
CH-1807 BLONAY
Tel.: +41 (0)21 943 26 73
Fax: +41 (0)21 943 36 05
E-mail: info@adeco.org
http://www.adeco.org

UNITED KINGDOM/ROYAUME-UNI
The Stationery Office Ltd
PO Box 29
GB-NORWICH NR3 1GN
Tel.: +44 (0)870 600 5522
Fax: +44 (0)870 600 5533
E-mail: book.enquiries@tso.co.uk
http://www.tsoshop.co.uk

UNITED STATES and CANADA/
ÉTATS-UNIS et CANADA
Manhattan Publishing Company
468 Albany Post Road
CRCTTON-ON-HUDSON, NY 10520, USA
Tel.: +1 914 271 5194
Fax: +1 914 271 5856
E-mail: Info@manhattanpublishing.com
http://www.manhattanpublishing.com

Council of Europe Publishing/Editions du Conseil de l'Europe
F-67075 Strasbourg Cedex
Tel.: +33 (0)3 88 41 25 81 – Fax: +33 (0)3 88 41 39 10 – E-mail: publishing@coe.int – Website: http://book.coe.int